Helping Children with Fear

Helping Children
with Feelings

Helping Children with Fear

Teenie Weenie in a Too Big World

A Guidebook

Margot Sunderland

Illustrated by

Nicky Armstrong

www.speechmark.net

Note on the Text

For the sake of clarity alone, throughout the text the child has been referred to as 'he' and the parent as 'she'.

Unless otherwise stated, for clarity alone, where 'mummy', 'mother' or 'mother figure' is used, this refers to either parent or other primary caretaker.

Confidentiality

Where appropriate, full permission has been granted by adults, or children and their parents, to use clinical material. Other illustrations comprise synthesised and disguised examples to ensure anonymity.

Published by
Speechmark Publishing Ltd
70 Alston Drive, Bradwell Abbey, Milton Keynes MK13 9HG, UK
Tel: +44 (0)1908 326944   Fax: +44 (0)1908 326960
www.speechmark.net

First published 2003
Reprinted 2004, 2009

002-5151/Printed in the United Kingdom/1010

British Library Cataloguing in Publication Data
Sunderland, Margot
    Helping children with fear – (Helping children with feelings)
    1. Fear in children 2. Anxiety in children 3. Emotional problems of children
    4. Problem children – behaviour modification
    I. Title II. Armstrong, Nicky
    155.4'1246

ISBN 978 0 86388 464 1

Contents

This book is accompanied by the childrens' story book, *Teenie Weenie in a Too Big World* by Margot Sunderland.

About the Author

MARGOT SUNDERLAND is a registered Child Therapeutic Counsellor, Supervisor and Trainer (UKATC), and a registered Integrative Arts Psychotherapist (UKCP). She is Chair of the Children and Young People section of The United Kingdom Association for Therapeutic Counselling.

Margot is also Principal of the Institute for Arts in Therapy and Education – a recognised fully accredited Higher Education College running Masters Degree courses in Integrative Child Psychotherapy and Arts Psychotherapy. She was founder of the project 'Helping where it Hurts', which offers free therapy and counselling to troubled children in several primary schools in North London.

Margot is a published poet and author of *Choreographing the Stage Musical* (Routledge Theatre Arts, New York and J Garnet Miller, England); *Draw on Your Emotions* (Speechmark Publishing, Bicester and Erickson, Italy); *Using Storytelling as a Therapeutic Tool for Children* (Speechmark Publishing, Bicester, awarded Highly Commended in the Mental Health category of the 2002 BMA Medical Book Competition), and the acclaimed *Helping Children with Feelings* series of storybooks and handbooks (Speechmark Publishing, Bicester).

About the Illustrator

NICKY ARMSTRONG holds an MA from the Slade School of Fine Art and a BA Hons in Theatre Design from the University of Central England. She is currently teacher of trompe l'œil at The Hampstead School of Decorative Arts, London. She has achieved major commissions nationally and internationally in mural work and fine art.

Acknowledgements

I would like to thank all the children, trainees and supervisees with whom I have worked, whose poetry, images and courage have greatly enriched both my work and my life.

INTRODUCTION

Who this book will help

✰ Children who worry a lot.

✰ Children exhibiting signs of ongoing anxiety.

✰ Children who experience the world as an unsafe place.

✰ Children who suffer from phobias or obsessions.

✰ Children who are emotionally overwhelmed by something they are finding far too difficult in their lives.

✰ Children who have nightmares.

✰ Children who are scared to tell someone that they are scared.

✰ Children who know a terrible loneliness.

✰ Children who feel insignificant in a world of adult giants.

✰ Children who need help in being assertive.

✰ Children who feel defeated by life.

✰ Children who feel so impotent that their only way to feel any potency is to be mute.

✰ That quiet little child at the back of the class who would not say boo to a goose.

WHAT LIFE IS LIKE FOR FEARFUL CHILDREN

If all the world's a stage, why can't I have a better part?
(Glouberman, 1989, p239)

Fear is a natural developmental stage, particularly around four to six years old, when a child's imagination is becoming very vivid, and at the same time they can think more deeply. At times, young children are convinced that there are monsters lurking in cupboards, under beds, or behind the stairs, just waiting for them – waiting to come out and pounce. This is quite natural. Objects and people can suddenly take on monster-like qualities – the eerie face found in the curtain material, the shadow cast by a jacket hanging on the back of the door. A 20-month-old infant screamed with terror on seeing a shoe with a floppy sole. Fifteen months later she was able to say to her mother in a frightened voice: 'Where are Mummy's broken shoes?' Her mother hastily said she had given them away and the child commented, 'They might have eaten me right up' (Segal, 1985, p34).

So, from time to time, all children will need help with feelings of being frightened and worried. But this book is about helping children for whom worry and anxiety have become a way of being in the world. For these children, being alive can seem like an unending struggle. These are children who never know real calm and never enjoy states of deep contentment or a sense that all is well in their world.

When children are persistently fearful, the world can seem a big and unpredictable place; threatening and dangerous. It is a world in which they rarely if ever feel safe; a world populated by people they cannot trust. This, coupled with a sense of self as impotent, helpless, always reacting, never being able to act, can feel to some fearful children like they are living a nightmare.

How a fearful child can move into a hiding, avoiding attitude to life

I found places where nobody else would ever go or want to go. And that's where I would go because nobody else would be there. And it would be nice and quiet. (Morton, 1995, p94)

Fearful children are often very resourceful when it comes to modes of flight and withdrawal, all designed as desperate attempts to make the unsafe world feel safer. Some stop talking and retreat into silence (selective mutism), trying to defend themselves from the demands of the outside world. Others retreat into a fantasy world of imaginary friends. (The child makes his own safe, imaginary people in contrast to the real, frightening people out there in his life.) Some fearful children hide from the world in very overt ways, spending hours on their own in their bedroom, or in front of the computer (computers being far safer and more predictable than people). Others literally run away from home or school, because it is just too painful to stay. Reality is experienced as far too difficult to tackle head-on.

Such children are not running *towards* anything. They are 'running away from'. But when a fearful child does find some effective way of

Figure 1

withdrawing or hiding, he never actually achieves a state of inner peace because he always has to re-enter the world of people at some point.

Statistics of child runaways (all under the age of 16)

An estimated 77,000 (one in nine) 14- to 15-year-olds run away from home each year, of whom 11,000 stay away for a week or more.

Research carried out by York University for the Children's Society suggests 100,000 children under 16 run away each year in the UK. A quarter first run away before the age of 11. Most of the young people running away from care had started running away before entering care.

There was no significant difference with respect to income level: young people were as likely to run away from better-off as from low-income families.

Of the young people who had run away from home, one quarter reported abuse, and one third left due to conflict with parents. Nearly one in ten left due to bullying or other school problems. (NCH, 2002)

Avoiding, hiding or running away can seem like the only option for a fearful child. He can experience the wish to leave or withdraw as an almost involuntary response: an urgent sense of 'I've just got to go/hide/say nothing.' The feeling of fear can be so strong that it overwhelms any thinking about possible alternative ways of dealing with the situation. The only option is to put as much distance between themselves and the threat as possible.

Many frightened children do not know that it is fear they are feeling. They only know they have a strong and desperate need to avoid new situations. So their protest is usually one of 'I don't want to' instead of 'I'm scared to'. Similarly some adolescents do not realise that what they are feeling is fear; they just know they have an overwhelming desire to stay in bed.

Oh no, I'm much happier in bed. Staying in bed suits me. I'd be very unhappy to get out of bed and go out and meet strangers and all that kind of thing. I'd really much prefer to stay in my bed. (Pinter, 1991, p53)

Flight is a normal animal behavioral response, a natural survival mechanism in the face of danger or conflict. It is of course entirely sensible and healthy to run away from situations of physical danger, be it a lion or a violent person. We also know that when the fear circuit in the subcortex of the animal brain is strongly stimulated (by electrodes) the animals have a motoric impulse to run away (Panksepp, 1998, p54). But, sadly, some children develop an attitude to life where flight has become their main response – often when there is no danger, and often when in actuality the person or situation is inherently very benign.

While a new challenge can fill the unfearful child with excitement, it fills the fearful child with dread. So life is sometimes kept narrow and safe in order not to venture beyond the familiar. Miss Havisham in Charles Dickens's *Great Expectations* talks to young Pip about Estella. His reaction tells us a great deal about how a sense of threat in the unfamiliar can quickly turn into the desire to run away.

> 'What do you think of her?'
> 'I think she is very proud,' I replied in a whisper.
> 'Anything else?'
> 'I think she is very pretty.'
> 'Anything else?'
> 'I think she is very insulting.'
> 'Anything else?'
> 'I think I should like to go home.'
> (Dickens, 1995, p51)

In being married to the safe and known such children can miss out on so much that is good and enriching in life – so much opportunity – because of this need to avoid anything they find even mildly stressful. They can end up missing the joys of relationship, shared adventure, laughter, fun and exploration. In fact, a situation evoking strong pleasurable feelings can feel just as threatening as one evoking strong negative feelings. It is the level of high bodily arousal that then becomes the threat.

Jane, aged thirteen
Jane remembers herself as a very anxious child. Her image of herself pre-10 was of a lump of lard. She remembers her parents constantly trying to persuade her to go outside and play with other children. Jane remembers watching these children having fun on the swings. Part of her wanted to join them, but she never did. The pull to stay in the safe familiarity of her bedroom and the kitchen was too strong. Now, aged 13, she said, 'At the time, I just knew that inside my house was where I wanted to be. Now I realise I was just terrified of going outside. But I hated myself for being so still and dead. I felt like a lump of lard.'

The truth is that children, just like adults, feel a lot better about themselves if they *do* tackle the new situation instead of running away from it. It can have a hugely positive effect on their self-esteem. A helpful book on this is appropriately called *Feel the Fear and Do it Anyway* (Jeffers, 1987).

How some fearful children choose to spend too much time on their own as a retreat from a frightening world

> Leaving is very primitive, it cuts off everything. (Resnick, 1993)

Some children who are frightened and anxious spend too much time alone. They prefer it that way. Clarkson (1989) makes a useful distinction between positive withdrawal and negative isolation. In positive withdrawal, a child chooses time alone for absorbed play or reading. It is a time not motivated by fear or avoidance. Hence it is a sign of health rather than a neurotic defence mechanism. As Rollo May (1976, p72) says, 'The constructive use of solitude… requires that we are able to be quiet, that we let the solitude work for us and in us. It is characteristic of our time that many people are afraid of solitude'. For children absorbed time alone can mean re-entering the world strengthened and nourished, and happy to see people again. Periods of daydreaming and play spent alone can be vitally creative for children, providing the necessary mind-space for all manner of imaginative things and ideas to be born – the five minutes gazing out of the window, the contented doodling, the absorbed colouring-in of a picture.

In contrast, if a child's time alone is motivated primarily by fear and the avoidance of others, it is called negative isolation. It is time used as escape – time that often makes the child more and more fearful about re-entering the world. All too often it simply reinforces a deep sense of inner loneliness, alienation and helplessness in a too-big world.

Emma, aged twelve

Emma was referred to a school counsellor as her teachers were very worried about her withdrawn behaviour. She had no real friends, and seemed to have no desire for any. In her first counselling session she made an image (Figure 2). It was an egg in a box surrounded by barbed wire. 'I wish I was the egg,' said Emma, 'an egg that would never have to hatch.'

Menacing eyes and killing looks — the fear of being seen or exposed

Eyes, channel between you and another person's inside, can hurt and pollute you. (Padel, 1995, p146)

Some children feel trapped in a world of people whom they expect will look upon them with judging eyes and critical thoughts. They can feel that there is no place to hide from these eyes and thoughts, no shelter, no getting away from this persecutory universe. Some fearful children avoid eye contact with people because they have a fear of being seen right into. Parents and teachers sometimes use shaming eyes as a disciplinary technique with children.

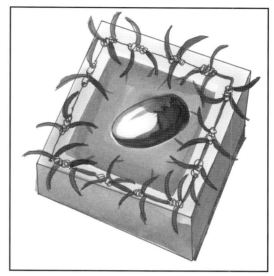

Figure 2   Drawing of Emma's sandplay story. (Emma was 12 years old.) 'I wish I was an egg in the box, an egg that would never have to hatch.' (The box was surrounded by barbed wire.)

Tony, aged six
'Her eyes might eat me all up,' said Tony, about his frightening teacher. Tony described his teacher as having X-ray vision, which made him feel dreadful.

It is clear that for some children, the feeling of being looked at by eyes that are judging, contemptuous, or icy-cold can have the effect of a physical blow:

They both had that eye thing, the one that pinned you and held you and sank right in, heavy and inert as lead. (Gibson, 1993, p99)

Philip, aged nine
Philip experienced one of his teachers, who regularly lost his temper, as very fierce and threatening. Philip became increasingly fearful. He started seeing faces coming out of the wallpaper to look at and taunt him. The familiar image in myth is that of Medusa, whose terrible gaze could turn people into stone.

One day, Philip said, 'I want to live on the moon because there are no people on it.' He started to not look directly into the face of any adult. He was obsessed with aliens 'that climb in through your eyes and live in your body.'

Outside the window a black rat
Sways on the briar like infected fruit:
'It looked me through, it stared me out, I'm not
Imagining things. Go you out to it.'
(Heaney, 1990, p117)

Fear kills play and can block the ability to learn, and the wish to explore the world

'… in the night, imagining some fear,
How easy is a bush supposed a bear!'
(Theseus in *A Midsummer's Night's Dream* 5 (1): 21–2)

Fear incapacitates. It can kill a child's capacity for play, spontaneity and creativity. In countries where there is famine or war, play is the first thing to go with children who are frightened. You simply cannot play or learn properly if you are very frightened. Your body-mind is on red alert. We know this from animal research. The fear circuit in the human subcortex has a very similar neuro-anatomy and biochemistry to other mammals' brains, with minor variations. (Interestingly, the fear circuit is bigger in rabbits than cats, and the rage circuit bigger in cats than rabbits.) In one experiment, a cat hair was placed near rats playing. The rats' play stopped totally for five whole days, even when the cat hair had been taken away. The room had become too associated with the cat hair (Panksepp, 1998, p19). Hence the power of Pavlovian conditioning! This is how powerful and toxic fear can be.

Fear can also totally override those systems in the brain concerned with the wish to learn and explore. So some frightened children will have learning difficulties, not because they have anything wrong with their brain, but because their fear is blocking their desire to learn.

A child who is frightened as a basic life position is often not free enough in his mind to feel curiosity, or to experience the urge to explore. His energies are taken up in being on guard and hyper-vigilant, and 'fending off'.

As the psychoanalyst Winnicott said, 'The [child] that is disturbed by being forced to react, is disturbed out of a state of *being*.' (1958, p xl). There is actually a biochemical reality to this in the brain. Too high levels of cortisol (a stress hormone) in the brain and body for long periods can block dopamine (a positive arousal chemical). Dopamine is vital for anyone to feel curiosity and eagerness to learn.

Fear also adversely affects a child's thinking capacity. The brain and body biochemistry of high states of fear cause a dramatic drop in IQ while the child or adult feels so under threat.

> A bad environment is bad because it becomes an *impingement* to which [the infant] must *react*. (Winnicott, 1958, p245)

How children who are not helped to feel and think about their fear will discharge it through action and/or physical symptoms

The bodily arousal of strong fear is extremely painful. Humans respond to it in one of three ways:

1   Finding someone to help them with their fear (this is called 'interactive regulation').
2   Moving into attempts to control it by action.
3   Discharging of the unbearable arousal.

If you do not do **1**, then **2** and/or **3** are inevitable.

The following are all attempts to *control* something frightening by action:

✰ Eating disorders

✰ Phobias (controlling something by moving away from it) – for example, school phobia

✰ Obsessions (controlling something by moving toward it)

✰ Selective mutism

✰ Worry or rumination

The following are all examples of *discharge* in a fearful child:

✰ Bed-wetting

✩ Vomiting

✩ Soiling

✩ Urinating inappropriately

✩ Nightmares

We will look at these in more detail in the next chapter.

Figure 3   When children are trying to manage what is scaring them all on their own, they often deal with their fear in one or more of the following ways: bed-wetting, soiling, compulsive rituals, vomiting or not speaking in certain environments (selective mutism). They may also develop phobias, obsessions, problems with eating and problems with sleeping. These are all attempts to deal on their own with the too-strong stress chemicals searing through their mind and body. They are trying to manage the unmanageable.

How fearful children often get into a 'lonely soldier' mode, and do not ask for help

> I would live happy
> in an ivy bush
> high in some twisted tree
> and never come out ...
> (Heaney, from 'Sweeney Astray'
> 1990, pp135–6)

One characteristic of many fearful children is not asking for help with what frightens them. They have become so locked in a regime of self-help that it never even occurs to them to ask for help from others. Fearful children can therefore fall into a habit of doing the hard things in their life all on their own. So if these children are being bullied, are struggling at school, or are really worried about something, they try to manage the situation and all their difficult feelings about it by themselves.

Gemma, aged twelve
Gemma remembered that when she was four she went to the cinema with her mother. She did not enjoy the film at all, as she spent the entire time worrying whether they would miss the bus home. Gemma never told her mother, who probably thought Gemma was enjoying the film.

Many adults cannot imagine that a child could ever have an anxiety disorder. After all, childhood is meant to be a carefree time, with none of the burdens of adult responsibilities. There is a vital flaw in this. Fears are exacerbated just as much by thoughts and images in the *internal* world as by the realities of *external* circumstances. This is just as true for children as it is for adults.

Some fearful children have good reasons for not asking for help with what is frightening them. For these children, experiences of comfort or solace have been all too few in their lives, or too weak, or too disappointing. So they cannot sustain any hope of a world that will listen, understand and actively support. Some fearful children have given up on relationships per se. This is a tragic position for a child to take, as we are all genetically programmed to need close supportive relationships with others if we are ever to know a true sense of calm and safety in the world. As Bowlby, the founder of Attachment Theory, says:

> Throughout adult life the availability of a responsive attachment figure remains the source of a person's feeling secure. All of us, from the cradle to the grave, are happiest when life is organised as a series of excursions, long or short, from the secure base provided by our attachment figures. (Bowlby, 1988, p62)

and:

> To stay in close proximity to, or in easy communication with, someone likely to protect you is the best of all possible insurance policies. (Bowlby, 1988, p81)

The Strange Situation Test by Mary Ainsworth is a test to ascertain the emotional security of one-year-olds. In the test, one-year-olds are put in what, for them, are high-stress situations, in which their mother leaves the room. As part of the test they are left for some time on their own and some time with a stranger. The emotionally secure child will cry when his mother leaves, and then seek comfort from her on her return. They are then quickly comforted. In contrast, some children do not cry when their mother leaves the room, and then when she returns they do not look for comfort. However, when the heart rates of these children are measured, it shows that they are just as distressed as the emotionally expressive children. It is simply that by the age of one, alarmingly, they have made the decision that when they are distressed and frightened the best thing is to deal with it by themselves. The studies also show that with these infants, their 'bottling up their feelings' mentality persists as they develop. Tragically, these children have not yet experienced the grown-ups in their life as a reliable source of comfort.

By and large, many fearful children have no or all too little concept of:

★ Asking for help when they are frightened.

★ The joys of togetherness.

★ Protest (saying no, or protesting in some other way, when someone is being cruel, harsh or coercive, or too pushy with them in some way).

★ A sense of their human rights as children.

★ Adults as being a reliable source of empathy, comfort and solace.

The need to be on guard at all times in this unsafe world

> Prudence itself demands that I should have a way of leaving at a moment's notice if necessary… All this involves very laborious calculation… for, despite all my vigilance, may I not be attacked from some quite unexpected quarter? I live in peace in the inmost chamber of my house, and meanwhile the enemy may be burrowing his way slowly and stealthily towards me. (Kafka, 1992, p130)

Kafka's 'mole' describes well the common hyper-vigilant behaviour often found in the fearful child. The fearful child cannot relax, because the terrible thing – whatever it is – might happen today, the next day, or the next. The future is something to be feared, not to be excited about. As the poet says, 'The blow that never falls batters you stupid' (Murray in 'Corniche', 1997, p19).

The following examples serve to show just how unsafe the world is perceived to be by fearful children.

Common emotional themes in the play, stories and artwork of fearful children

Figure 4 Depiction of a sandplay image by Hazel.

Hazel, aged eight
Hazel's mother was alcoholic. Her father had died of substance abuse. Her brother became a solvent abuser. Hazel was put on the Child Protection Register.

Hazel's story through play: The house is very wobbly. Spiders are coming in all over.* There is a baby hiding in the wardrobe. Even the fireman can't help the baby.** The baby gets killed off with snakes.

Common emotional themes
*Malign invasion.
**Help (the fireman) rendered impotent.

Simon, aged six

Simon's father flies into rages which makes Simon go very quiet and not speak for hours afterwards: 'Dad shouts at me, even if I say one word.'

Simon's play: There's a bug that eats everyone. Bug spray wouldn't kill the bug. If you stood on the bug, there would be an earthquake. The bug would be alive at the end of the earthquake but everyone else would be dead*.

Common emotional theme
*Total impotence in the face of an omnipotent destructive force.

Josey, aged nine

Josey was sent away to boarding school. She was locked in a cupboard when she was naughty.

Josey's story: There are silent people in the dark dungeon.* These people know hell. It's full of too alone. There is a castle with a very strong door to keep people out, but it won't work. The baddies will get in.**

Common emotional themes
*Impotence
**Hopelessness in the face of malign invasion.

Figure 5 Depiction of a sandplay image by Josey.

So often these fearful children speak in their play about tiny, impotent, defenceless creatures in the face of some omnipotent force of badness, cruelty, or lack of concern. This is all too true for children who have no sense that they have rights, do not know how to protest (or have lost any sense of protest they might have had) and who have no sense of their own anger, as their fear is all-consuming and eclipses any other feelings.

Manic defences: children who feel so small and frightened that they move into trying to feel big

The rest may be quite terrified, no more than a babe-in-arms, while this pretender, ... is up and out there, in the reeling world, wheeling and dealing with a great big name, fooling everyone in sight. (Herman, 1987, p27)

Some children who feel, or have felt, unbearable levels of fear and impotence move into a manic defence of pseudo-potency, which can come out in all manner of bravado. These are children whose fear is often accompanied by self-hate. They hate themselves for not being more assertive, more courageous. They start to hate anything wimpish in others, as they loathe it in themselves. These are the children who are attracted to sports like wrestling, kung-fu, etc, as a way to feel big and powerful when inside they feel quite the opposite. They may join gangs or bullies as a defence against their sense of themselves as so terribly isolated and fearful.

While some children do this in reality, others do it only in fantasy. Ian Fleming created the fictional James Bond character – one of the most able and powerful men imaginable – when he is said to have experienced himself in childhood as weak and feeble. In a similar vein, some fearful children have become counter-phobic. This means that unconsciously they are drawn to scary situations as an unconscious attempt to deal with their fear.

UNDERSTANDING HOW SOME CHILDREN DEVELOP A FEARFUL ATTITUDE TO LIFE

When a child's fearful attitude to life is a legacy from babyhood

a) When a child is fearful because the parent–baby dance did not go well

A baby is born into a world of relative giants. When the dance goes well between a parent and baby, the baby soon learns that the parent can comfort him and help him when he is very distressed. His parent becomes a shelter from things the baby finds frightening in the outer world. In contrast, when the dance does not go well, the baby learns that the parent herself is a source of anxiety or stress. Here are some of the ways in which this early dance can go wrong – often with very well meaning parents:

> [The parent] was pulling [the baby's] arm, picking him up to reach just his orientation, attempting to force his head in her direction. The infant dodged by moving back, ducking his head down, turning away, pulling his hand from her grasp, or by becoming limp and unresponsive... The infant also moved his head from one side to the other... with eyes squeezed shut. Thus, the infant's withdrawal behaviours influenced the mother to chase, and the mother's chase behaviours influenced the infant to withdraw further... Toward the end of the interaction, the infant increasingly lapsed into a limp, motionless head hang... (Beebe & Lachman, 1988, p324)

In-depth observations of parent and baby interactions (Murray, 1988; Beebe & Lachman, 1988) show that when a baby is too aroused by interactions with his parent, his excitement begins to feel uncomfortable, so he turns away from the parent in order to regulate his arousal level. Some parents do not understand or notice the disengagement, so they try to get the infant to re-engage. The infant turns away, but sometimes the parent then pursues him all the more. Some parents persist yet further in wanting the baby to interact with them – so much so that the baby eventually 'plays possum' to stop the contact between him and his parent. This interaction can happen as early as two weeks old. Beebe and Lachman call this interaction between mother and baby 'Chase and Dodge'.

Such a difficult relational start to life can leave a baby full of anxiety. The baby cannot manage the over-arousal caused by his mother – the very person who is supposed to protect him from stressful arousal. This early relational stress can then be transferred to other people (subconsciously), who are then feared as potential invaders, and seen as a threat to the very fragile sense of self.

Stella, aged six
Stella was a very anxious and withdrawn child. Using clay, she made a picture of a person with a big 'Keep Out' sign over her face. When Stella was a young baby her mother would repeatedly peer into Stella's cot, put her face too close to Stella, smother her with kisses, and jiggle her body up and down. Stella would start to cry.

This is called parental looming. Adults often forget how invasive they can appear to a baby when the baby has not yet formed an adequate defence system to fend off the (well-meaning) assault. The baby then puts all his energy into 'fending off' and not into building a strong self.

Figure 6 Stella, aged six, who was a very anxious child, made this figure in clay. She had experienced 'parental looming' in infancy.

b) Babyhood: When the dance goes wrong – the power of the too-strong parental face

> Please lend me your eyes.
> See what *I* see.
> *You* take it in,
> That I might look away.
> Just for a while.
> *Margot Sunderland*

For the baby, the world of sensation is vivid, undiluted and intense. So if what he sees or hears is too harsh or jarring in some way, he will experience it all too powerfully. This is largely to do with infant brain development. The part of the brain that can think about and process visual, kinaesthetic or auditory sensations is very underdeveloped after birth (this is called the pre-frontal cortex). So, just like someone who suffers from schizophrenia, the infant lives in a world of sensation that cannot be modified by thought. This means that sensations – sights and sounds – can be far too strong, and so can be experienced as very frightening very quickly. Faces and voices are particularly dangerous in this respect.

From about two to six months old the baby will be mesmerised by faces – particularly those of his parents. He can sustain eye contact for a long time without losing interest or wishing to look away. The problem arises when this so potent image of the parental face is too harsh a stimulus. Sometimes the baby sees something very angry, or hating, or despairing in the parent's face. It is too strong an image. At other times, the face is too blank. Lyn Murray's research demonstrates that when parents were asked to look blank at their babies, the babies got very distressed (1988).

It must be emphasised, however, that for the infant, relational stress of the frightening face is likely to leave a legacy of fear only if it is persistent, rather than a one-off or very occasional experience. It would be impossible for parents to modulate every nuance of their behaviour and expressions. But it is important to be aware how very transfixing an image the face is for infants – so if it is a frightening face, or too harsh or glowering, there can be long-lasting problems with relational stress.

Tony, aged eight

Tony's teachers said they themselves felt frightened when Tony's mother came to school to pick him up. She was full of rage, left over from her own abusive childhood: she had been beaten persistently by her father. She had found Tony a very difficult baby and said that she often screamed at him when he was crying. Now Tony would not look at adults when they spoke to him. He would shuffle his feet restlessly. When Tony went to The Natural History Museum in London, which was full of stuffed animals with glass eyes, he ran out on to the street in terror. When asked why he was so upset, he said, 'It's the eyes, they might have eaten me all up!'

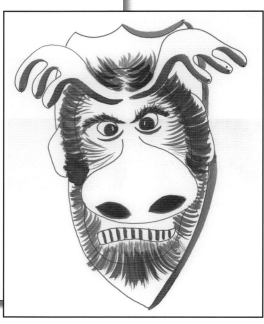

Figure 7 Tony: 'The eyes, they might have eaten me all up.'

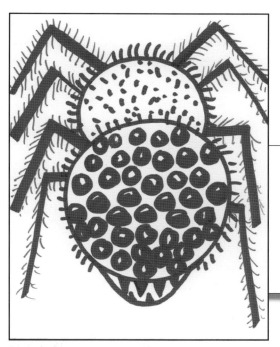

Jack, aged six
Jack's mother regularly glared at him with raging eyes. In therapy, he told this story: 'There's a black widow spider. It has 100 eyes. It shoots spikes from its eyes. People get frozen to the spot so they can't think any more.'

Figure 8 Jack: 'There's a Black Widow Spider. It has 100 eyes. It shoots spikes from its eyes.'

John, aged ten
John had nightmares of worms getting into his eyes. He told the therapist, 'I've always had dreams about black worms getting into my eyes.'

His mother also went into therapy. She said that when John was born she had suffered from post-natal depression, and on several occasions had indeed looked at him with murderous hate in her eyes. When she had worked this through, and talked to John about it, and said, 'I am so sorry if I ever frightened you', John's nightmares stopped. Up until then, John had never known why he never wanted to look directly into his mother's face, and had avoided eye contact with her whenever he could.

The following poem is written to convey the power of the too-strong, frightening face and shouting mouth of the adult, from the perspective of the helpless infant. The infant has not yet developed the defences to be able to fend off its impact, or distract himself from it in any way.

Face

These swelling eyes that shout with glare,
And vile looks floating by themselves,
And lips that flare alive with wrath,
All viper-quick with mad intent
That come so close with teeth and yell,
And bursts of speak in thudding tone,
Their sounds that rush into my skull,
And when they shout my head falls off.
Mummy I am dying here.

Mummy I'm being eaten up,
I'm scream and dread and shaking flesh,
And now it climbs into my face,
And sting its words into my eyes,
And fill my ears with death cold stare.
This face of horror is too strong,
I cannot blink or shut it out.

Mummy, let me hide in you,
And crouch against your warmth and skin,
And cling until they've all gone home,
Until it's you and me again.

Mummy please don't shut me out,
Mummy can't you hear my scream?
Mummy I am all in bits.
Won't you scoop me up again?
                                        Margot Sunderland

c) Infancy: When the dance goes wrong – the power of the too-strong parental voice

> Swooping witches and frightening teeth are released from the darkness of being unknown and unnamed. (Robbins, 1986, p124)

It is known that babies hate loud noises (their hearing is perfect in the third trimester of pregnancy). Babies often scream and scream on hearing a loud or frightening sound, as if the noise had got right inside them, and might send them quite mad. Remember that this world of sensation is so strong because babies cannot modify it through thought. Brian Keenan writes about the 'maddening' misery of enforced oppressive sound that you are helpless to stop. The extract below vividly conveys the baby's helplessness to do anything but endure the terrible sound of too-strong, jarring or harsh adult voices when his brain can not yet modify experience through thought or distraction.

> The constant fuzz and buzz and crackling screech bored into our heads like a needle. ... The mind was always drawn into it. It seemed to be inside us, recklessly slicing and gouging with a rusty broken scalpel. Every fibre and nerve of the body felt plucked and strained by it... It tore at the very membranes of the brain... It ate into you, devouring all sense and sensibility... Nothing would quell this crazy static... the noise was unbearable; how long could I endure this... my efforts only added to the torment. (Keenan, 1992, p148)

We know how sharp words can result in an infant collapsing in floods of distress, bursting into tears in shock. Even if the parent has acted in the child's best interest, in order to protect him from something, such as traffic or an electric plug, he still experiences her shout as an awful rupture in their relationship. He can seem to crumple and fall to pieces, physically and emotionally. He needs to be picked up and cuddled, as if in order to be put back together again. So the impact of shouting at an infant or child should never be underestimated. To him this adult is already a giant, and now a giant with a volcano of sound coming from its mouth. Coupled with glaring eyes, the impact can be far worse psychologically than a smack.

Of course, the best of parents will shout at a child from time to time. But what is important is whether they acknowledge the shock they may have caused, and whether they repair the situation? The psychotherapeutic word for this is *interactive repair*. Trauma only occurs to a child if there is no interactive repair. For example, if a child bursts into tears or wets himself as a result of the shouting parent, does the parent say, 'Serves you right', or move into ignoring him? This is traumatic, because there has been no interactive repair. But if the parent acknowledges the child's shock, apologises for causing it, and tries to comfort the child, it is very different. In the latter case, the child can be saved from a legacy of fear.

Danny, aged eighteen months

Danny fell to the floor in a desperate, sobbing heap when his mother shouted at him because he went too close to the fire. Danny was lucky, because his mother realised that her shout had meant he experienced a terrible rupture in his connectedness to her. So she scooped him up in her arms and 'put him back together again'. Children who have parents or teachers who regularly shout at them without interactive repair are far less fortunate.

Eric, aged three

In a rather expensive restaurant, Eric was merrily driving his Thomas Tank Engine into his spaghetti. His father shouted at him to stop. Eric burst into tears, got off his chair and ran over to his Daddy, climbed into his lap and sobbed and sobbed. Eric's father, realising that his voice had been too sharp and had been experienced by Eric as a terrible rupture between them, comforted his son. It showed the health of their relationship, that Eric confidently knew that his father would repair the situation.

Figure 9 Interactive repair

Three-year-old Eric, in an expensive restaurant, merrily drives his Thomas Tank Engine
into his spaghetti. His father is very angry, but then seeing how he has frightened
Eric, he repairs their relationship.

d) Babyhood: The monsters from within – how, without comfort and solace, the infant's own intense emotions and bodily sensations can be experienced as terrifying invaders

In moments of intense anxiety, or physical discomfort or pain, it is essential for a baby to feel soothed by a strong, calm mother-figure. Without this, when distressed he can all too easily feel overwhelmed by his feelings and bodily sensations. The intensity of these unmanaged feelings can be awful. Winnicott, a psychoanalyst, called them 'primitive agonies' (1965). Winnicott thought that anxiety was not a strong enough word. To the baby, 'primitive agonies' can actually feel like something *outside* of him attacking him, when in fact they are the shock and pain *inside* both his body and mind. Melanie Klein, a child analyst, wrote about this very eloquently. For example:

> The newborn baby experiences... anxiety of a persecutory nature... The young infant, without being able to grasp it intellectually, feels unconsciously every discomfort as though it were inflicted on him by hostile forces. (Klein, 1975b, p248)

Because the baby's mother is so central in terms of soothing or not soothing his distress, he can also feel intense rage if she does not respond. When he feels *the attack of the intensity of his rage* at his mother, he may feel that it is *she* who is attacking *him*. We know this from times when a mother has taken too long to come to her baby. When she does then approach, he can scream even more. His rage towards her, and his fear of the strength of his own rage, have become all muddled up in how he sees her, so now she is seen as frightening. He then needs to be picked up by Daddy or someone else, until in his mind Mummy becomes 'good' again. In psychoanalysis, this is referred to as 'persecutory anxiety'.

If a parent is defending herself against her own painful feelings, she will often be unable to manage effectively those of her baby. Consequently, she will not provide him with the protective shield he needs. In such cases, the baby's feelings can be experienced as monsters attacking him. They are, in fact, the monsters of his own unmanaged, uncomforted feelings.

Babies have no way of thinking about, understanding or distracting themselves from their pain (emotional and physical). They are unlike adults in this respect, who have plenty of opportunity for distraction – for example, books, television, ringing someone up, food, or talking to someone. The baby is alone, lying in his cot; he cannot get up and walk around. If his cries are not heard, or answered, he is left to deal with feelings that he cannot possibly manage. No wonder that an infant with such a start in life builds up a picture of the world as a threatening, frightening place.

Similarly, very painful, frightening and incomprehensible bodily sensations such as wind, hunger or teething pain can feel overwhelming to a small baby. A baby has no frames of reference within which to understand these terrible surges or agonies in his little body, and no reason to think they will not go on forever. *He just feels brutally attacked by something very frightening.* Again, without comfort and solace, this can contribute to the building up of a fearful attitude to life.

> The baby's rising crescendo of rage and fear as his hunger goes unsatisfied... [is experienced] as the rising threat of an increasingly hostile persecutor successfully attacking his tummy and making the pain worse and worse... The infant, right from the start, is beset by these situations in which he fears being damaged by something right inside him. (Hinshelwood, 1989, p35)

However, where an infant's terrifying feelings and body sensations can be soothed by the parent who can bear them, then the child can learn to bear them too, instead of learning to fear them. For those infants lucky enough to have such a parent figure, they will feel far stronger psychologically for not having to build up defences in childhood in order to deny, avoid, protect or defend against their too-strong feelings.

What is happening in the brain of the child who is locked in a fearful attitude towards life

Figure 10 shows the pre-frontal cortex. This is the higher functioning part of the human brain. The pre-frontal cortex is the part of the brain that enables us to think, reason and plan ahead, weigh up our options, calm ourselves down, and show concern for others. In humans the pre-frontal cortex has changed and grown in size dramatically in the course of our evolution. The lower brain, called the subcortex (the lighter shaded structures in the middle of the picture), is very similar to that of other mammals. This part of the brain has evolved relatively little. The lower brain is the part of the brain which triggers very powerful feelings in us, whether we like it or not. As humans, we might like to think that we do not have a primitive animal brain as well as our higher brain, but we do. As Panksepp, a neuroscientist, says:

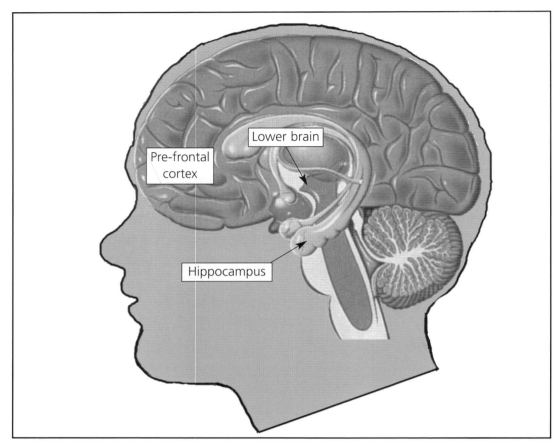

Figure 10 The emotional brain

> Ultimately, along came humans, who are prone to tell many tall tales, one of the most popular being that we are completely different from all the other species. (1998, p25)

It is the lower brain that triggers alarm signals of fear. These alert the body, which then serves to amplify the fear responses. These can be so strong that the higher, thinking brain (the pre-frontal cortex) can be hijacked too, so *all* thoughts are tinged with fear and alarm. If this happens, your IQ drops dramatically while under the influence of fear.

However, if the higher brain is functioning well, it can moderate a strong fear response and calm down both the body and the lower brain. It does this with soothing emotion chemicals and calming thoughts (the one triggers the other). In fearful children, the higher brain is not functioning well in terms of its stress-moderating capacity. We will look at why not, but first we will need to look more closely at some interesting neuroanatomy.

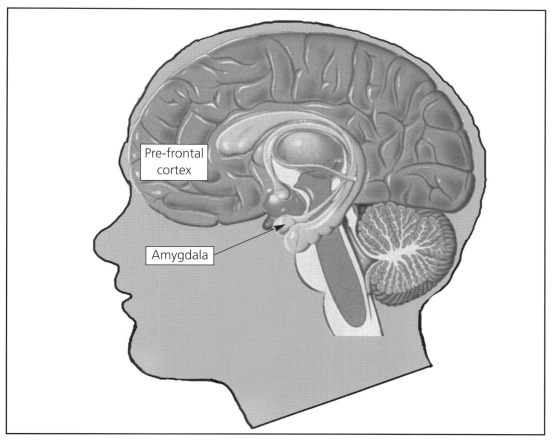

Figure 11   The amygdala

In the lower brain, one part of the fear circuitry is called the amygdala (see Figure 11). It is a small, walnut-shaped part of the brain, which can be located directly in from the ear. (There is one on either side of the brain.) The amygdala alerts us to threatening situations. If we perceive something as a threat, the amygdala triggers. This puts the brain and body on red alert – as if something in your brain has dialled the emergency number. The body prepares itself for fight or flight, so stress chemicals are released.

The amygdala is only doing its job. It reacts very quickly, and needs to assess, at speed, whether a risk exists. If a lion is chasing you, for example, you need a quick response, rather than thinking, 'How interesting, a beautiful animal with big teeth is running towards me.' Your amygdala says, 'Run!' A famous example, often quoted, is seeing a curved stick on the ground as you walk through a wood. Your amygdala will set off an internal alarm before your higher brain reveals that it is a stick, and not a snake. But it is important that it reacts that fast, as it may have been a snake! So, a chief function of the amygdala is being primed to sense anything that may be a threat to you, emotionally or physically. Conditioned fear responses to something or someone – for example, phobias – are again the amygdala at work. Damage to the amygdala in both animals and people commonly show up as having no fear in response to *actual* threats.

So what is going wrong in the higher and lower brain (the amygdala in particular) of the fearful child?

The problem for children who have known a lot of fear is that the amygdala will fire a lot, *even when there is no actual threat.* Why? Well, the amygdala is also one of the brain's many memory systems. It is an *emotional memory system.* If something in the present is remotely similar to something the child found frightening in the past, it triggers negative feelings and associations in his brain. So the amygdala can keep triggering memories of frightening images, sensations and impressions from the child's past.

The problem with the amygdala's emotional memory system is that it is a very 'sloppy system' – as Daniel Goleman called it in *Emotional Intelligence* (1996). This means that it generalises. So, for example, if a child was very frightened of an angry teacher with a moustache when he was five years old, then his amygdala can trigger all his life at men with moustaches, or indeed with all men in authority, and he is sent spinning into states of fear and threat.

The amygdala's alarm system is like an ill-fitted burglar alarm – it can go off at times when there is no actual threat. The more fear a child has known, the more likely is his amygdala to be trigger-happy. Each time an aspect of the fearful child's present situation reminds him of some emotionally painful image or event in his past, the amygdala can register it as *an actual repeat of that painful situation without the child actually knowing that he is remembering something!* That is the awful thing. When the amygdala fires because something in the present is slightly similar to something frightening in the past, the child's brain will not let him know he is remembering something. He will truly think his fear is totally justified by something in the present which is in fact perfectly benign.

If there's a real emergency – for example, a child faced with a violent father – then we need that sort of fast, hyper-alert reaction. But for the fearful child it is a huge burden when the amygdala keeps triggering alarm because it mistakenly thinks that something in the present is repeating pain and emotional threat from the past.

Sarah, aged twelve

Sarah had always been a very anxious child. On her first day at senior school, she was asked her name by a male teacher with a rather loud voice. From that day on, Sarah had been school phobic. On that first day, Sarah saw the teacher's eyes looking straight at her, and heard his loud voice asking her name. She had a sudden rush of anxiety. She felt hot and panicky and deeply shamed. For a while she could not answer, as if struck dumb, and she lost her capacity to think. In fact, throughout her childhood, many powerful male authority figures had had this same effect on her. Sarah's amygdala had triggered, so the fear circuit in her lower brain was highly activated. She was remembering something without realising it.

This is what had happened: when Sarah was three, her mother took in a lover who drank too much, and often became violent. Sarah had been scared out of her wits. The lover left, and yet the fear did not leave Sarah's brain. (It never would have, if Sarah had not had therapy to process it.) It had been stored as a terrible memory. Her amygdala had therefore been primed to watch out for such a threat, should it ever happen again. So every time a man spoke loudly Sarah's amygdala would trigger the unworked-through memory of her mother's lover's loud voice. This 'cluster' of *male authority figure–fixed look–name–booming voice* was enough of a sense impression for her amygdala to call 'Repeat! Repeat! Fear/Dread/Threat!' and to send her hurtling back to all the fear and shame she had felt in early infancy. So, in her senior school with this new male teacher, she had a massive psycho-biochemical stress response *before* her higher brain had time to properly process and think about the situation.

In therapy, she created a sandplay of her mother's lover as a terrifying monster face, and was helped by her therapist's empathy and attunement, and soothing and validation of her feelings, to process and work through the experience. Then male authority figures no longer had that terrifying effect on her. She still found them difficult, but her higher brain was able to act, and calm her down with ways of thinking and processing from her therapy sessions. Now she could say to herself, 'Whoops, remember you are just reminded of when you were three.' That thought was enough to stop her amygdala firing.

> The amygdala's emotional memories... are indelibly burned into its circuits. The best we can hope to do is to regulate their expression. And the way we do this is by getting the cortex (higher brain) to control the amygdala... [Psychotherapy is to help] the cortex [higher brain] gain control over the amygdala. (Le Doux, 1998, p265)

Why frightening experiences in early infancy are particularly lethal in terms of the amygdala

As the amygdala is virtually complete at birth, it also encodes early infantile sense memories of both pleasure and distress. In early infancy these are encoded in the brain *only* as *sense memories* and not as *event memories*. (This is because the parts of the brain that encode event memories are not fully established until later in development.)

In infancy, *sense memories* – that is, visual, auditory, olfactory, bodily, movement or energetic images – are formed from powerful reactions to things the infant sees, hears, smells and touches, and from energy states, etc. An *event memory* – a memory located in time and space – is a later developmental achievement. For example, a child remembers Mummy opening the door at night and coming into his room with an extremely angry face and voice, and wearing a blue furry dressing gown. If the infant was only six months old when this happened, then in later life he may simply trigger a frightening sense memory whenever he sees blue fur. He may have no idea why. This is because at six months old his brain was not developed enough to lay down an event memory.

Early frightening sense memories can easily be retriggered by something in the present. The child unexpectedly has a sudden, strong reaction to some seemingly (from an adult's point of view) very minor thing – like a blanket, or going into a tunnel. Or he feels a rush of fear on seeing an expression on someone's face, and has no idea why. It may be the smallest of happenings that re-triggers some past fear, sending him into a sense of dread. Bollas (1987, p6) (a psychoanalyst) termed these triggers the 'unthought known'. You *know* these things, have *felt* them, *but you have not yet thought them*. As these sense memories were laid down in infancy, they are raw sensory images never translated into thought (because the infant did not yet have the brain wiring to encode that sort of memory – an event memory).

This explains some childhood phobias, when a child feels inexplicable terror of some very benign object for seemingly no reason – for example, feathers, pigeons or trumpets. An early infantile sense memory – auditory, kinaesthetic, tactile, or visual – is probably being triggered.

Because of the way the brain is hard-wired, it is vital that adults take on board the lethal power of fear

It is very important not to frighten children, as fear can hard-wire an oversensitive and trigger-happy amygdala. This means it keeps firing 'Threat!' at even the smallest stressor, which a non-fearful child would just take in his stride. In other words, the brain can be hard-wired in childhood for a fearful, anxious response to life. As we shall see, this can be caused by a whole range of stressors, not just major traumas like the death of a parent or a car accident. A stressor can be, for example, a repeatedly angry parent, a repeatedly anxious parent, a shaming teacher, or some bullying siblings.

Setting up stress-moderating systems in the child's brain – the vital role of helping a child when his amygdala has triggered a fear response

If a child is consistently helped with his fear then, over time, the higher brain can come online and calm the trigger-happy amygdala. This is how it works: if a child is consistently soothed and calmed when his amygdala has fired fear and threat, then, over time, stress regulatory systems will be established in his higher brain. This means that in times of stress, stress-moderating chemicals will be released from his higher brain to his lower brain, via the vehicle of reassuring thought. It is as if the brain is saying, 'We do not need to keep pumping out all these powerful stress chemicals; there is no real emergency here.'

Once the higher brain has established a stress regulatory system it can override those raw responses from the amygdala in the lower brain, screaming 'ALARM, ALARM'. However, if there is not enough soothing, empathy and understanding of a child's fearful feelings in childhood, these vital stress-moderating pathways from the higher to the lower brain will not be properly established.

Tragically, some people never properly establish these stress-managing systems in their brains, so they never enjoy this wonderful human resource of

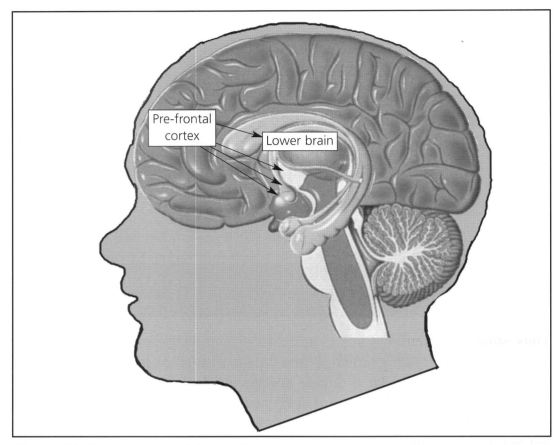

Figure 12 Emotional regulatory pathways

If a parent is a reliable 'emotional regulator' for her child, lifelong stress regulating systems will be established in the child's brain. Brain pathways will be formed from the pre- frontal higher brain to the lower more primitive mammalian brain. This means that any fearful impulse (which we all have from time to time) can be thought about instead of simply discharged.

being able to calm oneself down when stressed or anxious, or of being quickly soothed by a reassuring other. For them, fear, anxiety and agitation become ingrained personality characteristics. As adults, these 'unhelped children' are often exhausting to be around. Their energy is hyper and agitated. They have simply not established an anti-anxiety chemistry in their brains. They are tormented by persistent states of agitation and fear, which in turn torment the people in their company!

Because of the higher brain's plasticity, it is never too late for the brain to establish an anti-anxiety chemistry and stress-regulatory system – but this requires very powerful therapeutic input, often including re-parenting experience. More details about will be found in the chapter 'Considering Counselling or Therapy for Fearful Children'.

Children who have known so much horror or terror that natural numbing devices take over in their body-mind – some then move into terrifying others instead

Some children have suffered such repeated, gross and terrifying trauma that their body and brain move into natural numbing and cutting-off defences. This means that they move from a state of hyper-arousal to hyper-inhibition. The level of terror, the persistent triggering of the amygdala and terrible bodily arousal have become so unbearably painful that the brain-body system simply cuts off. The same mechanisms can be found in animals in the most extreme circumstances. The mind and body of a wildebeest, for example, will move into this state of numbness when in the jaws of a lion. If, for some reason, it manages to escape, its body will move back into extreme hyper-arousal and involuntary shaking.

Thus some children who have been terrified out of their wits can seem impervious to fear. What has happened is that the bodily arousal system – via an overactive parasympathetic part of the autonomic nervous system (the vagal nerve) can indeed shut off painful bodily responses of fear, so the child feels very little. The body also releases numbing opioids. Vital muscles in the gut tense, so that body-brain communication is dramatically stifled.

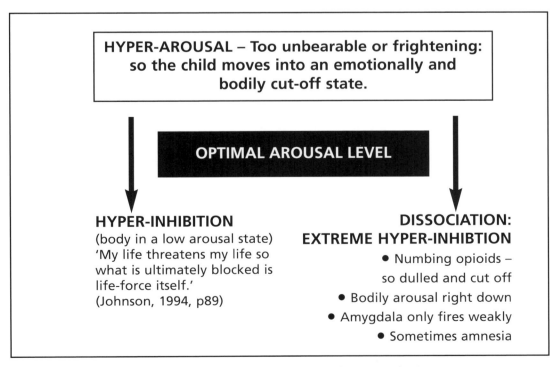

Figure 13   Defences when the intensity of arousal feels too frightening

Hence some traumatised, terrified children can then be horrendously cruel to another child or animal. Subconsciously, they act out their own trauma. They no longer remember their own fear. They are under-aroused, not over-aroused. Serial murderers who have suffered as children in this way, and who go on to kill in a cold and calculated manner, have far weaker amygdala firings than average. Their body is in a state of low arousal, often heightened by numbing opioids. This means they can slit someone's throat and feel little.

But if these so terribly damaged children are given therapy in which they really trust the therapist, they can 'thaw', and then their unbearable levels of anguish surface once again. Tragically however, if these children are left unhelped right into adulthood, the story is often a very different one. Research shows that giving therapy to serial killers in fact just makes them worse. So there is all the more reason to reach these terrorised souls, and help them when they are still children.

The brain hard-wiring power of the frightening grown-up — how relational stress is arguably the most frightening thing for a child

Figure 14 The brain hard-wiring power of the frightening grown-up.

I can never look forward to a new day, because it might have frightening people in it. (Elaine, aged twelve)

Research shows that *relational trauma and stress* – that is a known person being cruel or frightening to a child – is far more likely to provoke post-traumatic stress than natural disasters (Scurfield, 1985, pp219–56). This is understandable because in natural disasters people often pull together; they support and empathise with each other. Whereas in relational trauma, when someone is being cruel or frightening to a child – particularly a parent-figure who is supposed to protect them – the child is left with a terrible sense of aloneness, helplessness, betrayal and broken trust. Relational stress can have enduring consequences for later life, as we shall see.

Children who have suffered persistent experience of adults as angry, critical or harsh, can feel like putty in those giants' hands – helpless, powerless, without words or voice, and importantly without a will. Being with a fierce giant can provoke a sense of impending doom; a life of reacting to the storms of the 'monster' adult, with no sense of being able to act, protest, or indeed ask for help from a kind adult. Many children do not even consider protesting, because this could aggravate the 'giant' even more, putting them at even greater risk of retaliation. Whatever you do, you must not upset the angry giant!

Living in a world with a frightening, angry adult in it can be enough for a child to believe that the world is full of malevolent giants. (Remember, we can't stop the amygdala generalising from the specific.) As a result other adults are met with great mistrust, as if they all might be monsters posing as people.

> In the night, imagining some fear,
> How easy is a bush supposed a bear!'
> (Theseus in *A Midsummer's Night's Dream* 5 (1): 21–2)

So, when a child's life is blighted by regular contact with a frightening grown-up – for example, a teacher, parent, relative, etc – he can develop a *fear* of life rather than a *love* of life. Furthermore and tragically as we have seen, if too much of a child is given over to being hyper-vigilant in case of attack, there can be too little left for development of the self. Then, without sufficient warm, kind and empathic interactions with others, the child's emotional development can be arrested.

> He is detached from life rather than participating in it... He would emerge into social life for a brief foray in order to get a 'dose' of other people, but 'not an overdose'. (Laing, 1967, p53)

Living with the volcanic parent

> Another affliction –
> the witch-bird swooping down from the high crags
> the Sphinx screeching out of the sky
> clinging with clawed hands and clawed feet
> to the ramparts
> snatching away our children
> off into the untrodden blue.
> (Chorus in Euripides, *The Phoenician Women*, 1994, p81)

Figure 15 Living with a volcanic parent can hard-wire the brain for an overactive fear circuit.

Children are often acutely aware of cold, angry or hating feelings in their parents. Dorothy Bloch's excellent book *So the Witch Won't Eat Me* (1978) is full of stories of children who sense with amazing accuracy the raging and sometimes murderous feelings of their parents. It is perfectly common for parents to have occasional murderous feelings towards their offspring. As all parents know, all children at times are totally and utterly exasperating. The problem arises, however, when such feelings are persistent rather than occasional.

Young children cannot effectively defend against feeling the full force of raw, unprocessed negativity from their parents. Atmospheres of hate or rage – spoken or unspoken – can be as powerful in establishing a fearful attitude to life as can actual abuse or traumatic loss. The psychoanalyst Heinz Kohut makes this point:

> There is no doubt that gross events – such as the births, deaths, illnesses, and deaths of siblings, the illnesses and deaths of parents, the break-ups of families, the child's prolonged separations from the significant adults, his severe and prolonged illnesses, etc. can play an important role in the web of genetic factors that lead to later psychological illness. But clinical experience tells us that in the great majority of cases it is the specific pathogenic personality of the parent(s) and specific pathogenic features of the *atmosphere* in which the child grows up that account for the mal-developments, fixations, and unsolvable inner conflicts characterising the adult personality. (Kohut, 1977, p187)

If a child is perpetually frightened by a parent – *the very person he needs as protector* – it will be very difficult for that child to lay down firm foundations in terms of a deeply held sense of safety or security about being in the world.

Martha, aged nine

Martha had a recurring nightmare, in which she was running away from a dark figure who was always waiting for her in the place she ran to. She also had nightmares of him standing over incubator babies, and turning off the machine, so they died.

During her time in therapy, Martha's mother told the therapist that, due to post-natal depression and exhaustion from working long hours, she had often experienced murderous feelings towards Martha, and would scream at her when she was a baby and later when she was a toddler. When Martha's mother found a way to tell Martha that she was sorry if she had been frightening to her, Martha stopped having nightmares.

> This hag had to lie in a certain way
> At night lest the horrible black angular hatred
> Poke through her side and surprise the pretty princess
> Who was well deceived by this posture of love.
>
> (Hughes from 'Hag', 1970, p46)

Sally, aged ten

Sally's mother had been violent towards her children on several occasions, and Sally would physically shake if anyone raised their voice in the classroom. In play therapy, Sally repeatedly drew pictures of very cruel monsters and poisonous plants. She said to her therapist, 'You threaten me with a belt and say you'll smash the living daylights out of me unless I eat my food.' She repeatedly said, 'I'm a good girl, I'm a good girl.' Whenever Sally played with dolls she wanted to pull off their heads. She said, 'I'm 10 and my brain is shrinking.'

Emotional theme: Sally reenacted through play how she had been treated, in an attempt to try to work through this – for example, 'You threaten me with a belt, etc.' The cruel monsters and poisonous plants depict her sense of a very malign world.

Tragically, Sally saying her brain was shrinking had some truth in it. Exposure to persistent relational stress can cause actual cell death in the hippocampus, a key memory system in the brain (see Figure 10). This shows up on brain scans as a shrunken hippocampus. (We do not know yet to what extent a shrunken hippocampus might lead to a child experiencing learning difficulties.)

Nicky, aged eleven

Nicky, whose father had an alcohol problem and was always exploding with rage, enacted stories in therapy. She said, 'Someone gives up and wants to die. Planes try to come and help, but they all break apart on the way there. A baby drowns – nobody hears him calling. The wind blows out the little wind, until there is no little wind.'

Emotional themes: Nicky is communicating about unanswered cries for help; help rendered impotent; giving up; and not making it, all in the context of a very frightening world.

Gemma, aged six

Gemma's father was violent and alcoholic. His wife locked him out when he was drunk, but he banged on the door to be let in (sometimes repeatedly, for hours). Gemma's statements in therapy included: 'Can we play at Sellotaping up the door again?' When asked by the therapist where she would most like to be in the world, she said, 'In a locksmith's.'

Emotional theme: Gemma is communicating about her traumatic fear of invasion.

John, aged eleven

John's mother had dramatic mood swings and violent outbursts, and John feels impotent in the face of his mother's anger.

John says: 'I'm making a Venus Fly Trap to take the bad people and keep them prisoners.' (Perhaps he wants to trap the danger that is his mother's anger. Then he can be in control of it.)

His next statement shows vividly both the futility, and often the danger, of asking for help from volcanic parents:

'The pig was being drowned. When he called out for help, his head was chopped off.'

The teachers were very worried about John. He was a loner who seemed to find his own fantasy world far more appealing than the real world of inter-personal relationships.

Because the child suffering from acute relational stress cannot actually leave the frightening family home, he may learn to use his imagination for flight fantasies. In fantasy, he plays at being powerful, or being helped by someone powerful like Superman. These can become vital psychological retreats that enable him to escape for a time from the unbearable.

A psychic retreat comes to represent a place where respite from anxiety is sought and this is achieved by a greater or lesser divorce from contact with reality. (Steiner, 1993, p88)

Living with the parent who hits – the legacy of fear

If the... demand is made by a witch or giant whose features are distorted with rage, whose voice smashes through all the defences of the child's mind, and whose hand is ever ready to strike humiliation and terror into his face and head, it requires enormous therapeutic power to neutralize this programming. (Berne, 1979, pp116–17)

Without exception, all the adults I have met who were beaten as children, and who have not been in therapy, carry an anguished level of emotional and physical intensity when stressed or threatened. This is the legacy of knowing unbearable levels of emotional and physical intensity in both themselves and their parents, alongside abject feelings of both terror and betrayal.

Trudy, aged eight

Eight-year-old Trudy was beaten regularly by her mother. Her trauma had left her with a legacy of:

✫ Not being able to trust
✫ Hyper-vigilance
✫ Startle reaction
✫ Trigger-happy amygdala
✫ No friends

No-one wanted to be with her. She was too much like a tornado. In therapy she said: 'Wolves make a noise like your Mum trying to kill you.'

Maria, aged seven

Maria was taken into care because of the violence she suffered at the hands of her psychotic mother, who heard voices instructing her to punish Maria. Here are Maria's stories:

✫ 'Cruella de Ville married Herod from the Bible, and together they killed all the babies and all the Dalmatians.'
✫ (On Cruella de Ville) 'She is really loud and then a bit crazy, and then there is a crash and that's it.'
✫ 'A wizard is cooking all the children.'
✫ 'Snow White is too frightening a story, because the woman is too bad. I can't listen to it any more.'
✫ Maria said in one therapy session, 'Can I have a spot for killing in the session?' Her therapist asked, 'Who do you want to kill?' Maria replied, 'I have two mothers, one is not my mother and the other one is dead.'

Freddie, aged six

Freddie's mother beat him. Freddie would throw his arms around his teacher and say, 'I want to kill you and have you got a Mummy, I haven't got a Mummy.'

Sam, aged six

Sam's mother beats him. Here are Sam's stories:

✰ 'The witch is glad because she's scaring somebody.'
✰ 'The gorilla puts his hand over his mouth. He can't speak, because if he did he might say, "Why me?"'
✰ He drew a tiny figure on a huge piece of paper. 'The paper will gobble him up,' he said. Then, 'I'm not scared of anything.' Two minutes later he said, 'I'm scared of everything.'
✰ 'If I get paint on me, my mother will hit me.'

Parental violence – the legacy of fear for the child witness

For a child to witness their beloved mother being brutally attacked leaves them feeling terrified, unprotected and desperately alone with the agony. They need her to help *them* with *their* feelings, and yet of course she cannot. Without help with their feelings, in the form of counselling, therapy or a very good listening teacher, these children will not escape psychological scarring. The trauma of witnessing parental violence is just too horrific. A world with parental violence in it, is a very unsafe world indeed.

As Miller says:

A child cannot understand why the woman who in his eyes is a giantess in actuality fears her husband as if she were a little girl. A child cannot help but suffer from this.' (1987, p192)

Julie, aged six
Julie witnessed both parents attacking each other on a regular basis. These are the stories Julie played out in therapy:

- She played the high end of the piano and asked, 'Does this sound like screaming?'
- 'Everything is horrible in the cupboard.'
- 'The ants are too small, the giant is too big.'
- 'There's a terrible fire in the house that never goes out.'
- 'People are being nice when the visitors come, but actually everyone is dying in the basement.'
- 'Other people's anger gets put in my room.'

Emotional themes: the terror, the horror, the unbearable intensity (the image of fire), the hopelessness, the importance, the deceit of the 'all-is-OK' façade.

Living with the sexually abusing parent – the legacy of fear

> For the incest survivor the world is a dangerous place, period. It is not dangerous this or that time, or for this or that reason; it is simply unsafe. (Blume, 1990, p126)

In many cases of childhood sexual abuse, particularly when there is a threat against telling, the trauma can generalise in the mind of the abused child to a fear of all situations of intimacy and closeness. A child's perception of what it is like to be in the world, can be completely altered by the experience of sexual abuse. This is particularly the case when the abuser is a parent – the very person who is supposed to protect you. Blume talks of the adult still being locked in fear from the legacy of childhood sexual abuse:

> One after-affect is a 'disappearing act'. Incest survivors sometimes 'drop out of sight', not returning phone calls, not going to meetings or socialising, making themselves totally unavailable. This hiding is not the same as being alone or learning to feel comfortable in one's own company; it is extreme in its totality. Avoiding others, isolating oneself, while growth inhibiting, can be effective methods of protection. (Blume, 1990, p127)

Some eating disorders in children who have been sexually abused originate from a basic fear of 'taking in' – as what was taken in was highly toxic and dangerous. Gianna Williams writes about this profoundly as the phenomenon of 'No Entry defences' in her book, *Internal Landscapes* (1997). These children may also grow up with a wish for locks on all doors, as well as all manner of other metaphorical or literal 'No Entry defences' in neurotic symptoms.

Many sexually abused children suffer from post-traumatic stress, which means that they are constantly on red alert. They react with a startle reflex to anything that their brain 'reads' as a reminder, or has aspects (however small) that are similar to the original abuse. Sexual invasion can be experienced by some children as being stolen from – from their body, their innocence. It can leave them with a hopelessness about ever being able to maintain *any* privacy or protect their body boundaries again.

Terry, aged fifteen

Terry was sexually abused on many occasions by his father, and was taken into care. He rigged up no less than 17 handmade burglar alarms inside his room: he had too often been 'broken into' in his life. He was obsessed with controlling his circumstances, because in the past he had been unable to do so. His physical space had been so badly invaded by his abusive father that he reacted by manically protecting himself from any analogous intrusions.

Edward, aged twelve

Edward was sexually and physically abused by his father, so he had to be put into care. This picture depicts how Edward felt when his social worker came to wake him up in the morning to ask him to get up. When I asked him which of the monsters depicted his social worker, he said, 'All of them.' His social worker was actually very quiet and unassuming. (The problem was that Edward's amygdala was generalising: his fear of his father was generalised to all men everywhere.)

Figure 16 Edward, age 12, was diagnosed with post-traumatic stress after suffering abuse at the hands of his father. This meant that he generalised from the specific. So all men everywhere became frightening to him. This is Edward's perception of his male social worker who came to wake him up. He is the little figure in the bed.

Some children who have been sexually abused have fears of contamination. This is, of course, understandable, as something terrible did 'get in'. One sexually abused child I worked with in therapy spent session after session taking out the little bits of shell from the sand in the sandbox. She said they were making the sand poisonous. She had real trouble eating anything in case someone had poisoned it. (No entry defences.) She could not get on with living, because her fears were so strong.

> I've been polluted
> By the touch of a traitor.
> All my bright hopes
> Fallen to dust.
> (Euripides, *Medea*, 1994, p21)

Why disciplining and socialising a child is a real art — and how it can far too easily result in a child developing a fearful attitude to life

> The idea of a lot of no one appeals to me. I'd like very much... to go on an excursion with a whole crowd of no one. Into the mountains, of course — where else? (Kafka, 1981, p24)

Children are not born socialised. They all need to be socialised — for example, to learn that to hit the boy next door; to sit on the baby's head, or to poke the cat in the eye, is unacceptable. But the way this is done is very important if a child is to avoid developing a fearful attitude to life.

Some parents and teachers argue that disciplining children comes very naturally to them. The problem is that what comes naturally to them is often the way they themselves were disciplined by *their* parents. Hence the classic statement, 'I smack my child. It never did me any harm.' Some teachers and parents use disciplining methods that do indeed stop a child's unacceptable behaviour, but at far too high a price. The child is left with oversensitive amygdala and a trigger-happy fear circuit in his lower brain.

Think of some of the most common ways of disciplining children, used for decades: the looming-over; the shaming eyes; the shouting; put-downs; criticisms; the suddenness and shock of raging outbursts; the smacking, caning, and throwing of the blackboard rubber. Equally traumatic is the experience of public exposure – of being told off in front of the whole class, of punishments that deliberately humiliate and shame.

Charlie, aged eight

Charlie told his mother he hated getting up in the morning because being with his classroom teacher felt like entering a monster's cave. Charlie's mother moved him to a more benign school. But tragically, too many children with over-strict teachers tell no-one of their fears, and just grin and bear it day after day after day. It never occurs to them to ask for help.

Shame and fear at school in relation to performance and learning feel so acute for some children that they are subsequently terrified about handing in assignments, or about going near a computer, or picking up a paintbrush or musical instrument. In adult life, some are left with a fear of learning situations per se. What is happening is that their amygdala is still triggering childhood memories of the original shaming experiences around learning.

Neuroscientists have shown that, as a traumatic memory is triggered, the very same release of stress hormones, as happened originally, can happen again. Such stress hormones are so powerful that the child or adult is left unable to think properly. The body is prepared for flight or fright and the higher brain is awash with stress chemicals. The IQ then literally drops dramatically. Some adults are still extremely incapacitated in this way.

Philip

As a child, Philip was shouted at relentlessly during tea-time – that he wasn't holding his teacup properly – as his father tried to help him learn social etiquette. When he grew up he was terrified that he would be offered a drink in new social settings. He could not bring the cup to his lips without uncontrollable hand-shaking.

Many adults forget that children have not yet formed a strong self, or a protective defence system: as a result, many children cannot deal with criticism or angry attacks, proffered in the name of discipline, without becoming traumatised by them. Parents and teachers often do not realise just how vulnerable some children are to the effects of put-downs and angry faces and voices.

When socialising a child includes making them believe that you know everything they are doing

Some parents shout, '*I know exactly what you're thinking!*', or outside the child's door, '*I know what you're doing in there!*' Others teach their children about a judgemental god in the sky who witnesses everything they do or think. As a result, some children are left believing that their parents, or God, can get right into their mind. It is a terrifying belief, leaving them unable to feel safe in the world.

> Curse not the king, no not in thy thought; and curse not the rich in thy bedchamber: for a bird of the air shall carry thy voice, and that which hath wings shall tell the matter. (The Bible, Ecclesiastes, 10: 20)

Why shaming a child in the name of discipline can have a negative effect in terms of hard-wiring an overactive fear response in the lower brain

So farewell – to the little good you bear me.
Farewell, a long farewell…
(Cardinal Wolsey in *Henry VIII* 3(2): 351–2)

Some children develop a persistently fearful and anxious attitude to life because they have been shamed in the name of discipline; perhaps humiliated, mocked, or exposed in some cruel or belittling way. Shaming has such a negative effect, psychologically and neurobiologically, that the child can become 'people-phobic'. Then, apart from a safe and known few, all too many people the child meets, can be seen as potential shamers (the amygdala generalising from the specific again). From the fear of more shame, the child finds himself avoiding new social situations. He soon learns to prefer 'peopleless spaces'.

Children who live in fear of shame are often very good, over-compliant children. And so they can go through school life unnoticed in terms of needing help from a school counsellor or therapist. As Mollon says:

> Because [shame] evokes the wish to hide and to protect the self, shame by its very nature tends to be hidden. (1993, p52)

An exception was Tom, aged seven, who started bed-wetting after changing to a new school. He went to see a school counsellor. In therapy, he told the following story: 'The big fish with teeth is glad because she is scaring somebody.' After a while, it was clear the 'big fish with teeth' was how he was experiencing his new teacher. The problem was brought to the attention of the head teacher. The teacher was confronted and Tom stopped bed-wetting.

'Mummy is good. It's just other people and things I am frightened of' – when the child denies that their parent is frightening, so the fear gets displaced onto other people or things

Internally she is alone with persecutors. (Anderson, 1992, p100)

A child with a frightening parent can go through life feeling fearful, without allowing himself to know that it is his parent he is frightened of. Instead, he develops all manner of phobias, obsessions or physical symptoms.

It is often only when these children reach adulthood and with therapeutic help, that they really let themselves know they were frightened of a parent. It would have been too awful to let themselves 'know' their fear in childhood. As we have seen, it is a mad and maddening situation for a child to let himself know that he is frightened of the very person who is supposed to be protecting him. So denial or desensitisation of his fear of a parent is arguably a very sensible defence.

However, the problem is that the denied feelings of fear towards a frightening parent are then transferred on to other things or people. As Freud rightly said, feelings pushed into the unconscious 'proliferate [there] in the dark' (1979a, p148). The child's inner world is then populated by frightening images. As a result, the child may develop a phobia or obsession which serves to express his fear. In other words, repressing feelings of fear does not get rid of the feelings, it just diverts them.

Dorothy Bloch's book *So the Witch Won't Eat Me* (1978) is about the child's fear of infanticide. It relates case upon case of children who lived in fear that a parent would kill them. Bloch repeatedly found that in therapy these children wanted to enact fleeing from a fierce monster. But Daddy and Mummy were never actually identified *as* the monster.

> Children's fantasies appeared to concentrate on the fear of being killed, but the displacement of terror onto monsters and imaginary creatures was obviously designed to preserve an idealised image of their parents, from whom it was therefore possible to receive the love so essential for their survival. (Bloch, 1978, p12)

In other words, the child tells himself, 'Mummy is good, it's just the other people who are terrifying.'

Understanding childhood phobias

> Please somebody help me get rid of everything in my mind. (Rowe, 1988, p12)

There are two types of phobias – associative and symbolic. An *associative phobia* is the product of an association with something traumatic in the child's past *that actually happened*. A *symbolic phobia* is when the thing feared is a *metaphor* for something in their past. This is a vital distinction.

Many books on fears and phobias talk at length about associative fears, and entirely leave out fears and phobias that have a metaphorical reference to something in the past, but which did not actually take place.

Table 1 shows the differences between associative and symbolic phobias.

Understanding how a child can develop phobia

A phobia is when anxiety or fear has attached itself to a particular object or event. The child's level of fear around this thing or event is so high that he wants desperately to avoid it. It is a sense of 'If I do not avoid this terrifying thing, my level of anxiety would become unbearable.'

A phobia is very much like a nightmare. The only difference is that you are awake. Nightmares and phobias each contain very frightening images of threat and danger. In both, there is heightened imagining of the worst and a heightening of feelings of helplessness. In both, the imagined catastrophe is perceived as a *certain* catastrophe.

TABLE 1: THE VITAL DIFFERENCE BETWEEN AN ASSOCIATIVE PHOBIA AND A SYMBOLIC PHOBIA

An associative phobia is where something really frightens a child because it is associated with an actual event.

So, if bitten by a dog, a child may then be phobic of dogs. His phobia generalises to all dogs everywhere, instead of just the kind of dog that bit him. (Remember the generalising properties of the amygdala.) Whatever the child is *perceiving strongly at the time of the trauma* (for example, the dog's teeth or fur, etc) makes a deep link in his mind with the terrible feelings he experienced.

> **Toby, aged four**
> Toby had been attacked by a dog when he was four. He had tried to grip its fur, in vain, in order to fend it off. He was scratched, but was more shocked than actually hurt. No-one helped Toby talk about and work through his feelings about this trauma. They just said 'Kiss it better', put a bandage on the scratches, and 'Now go out and play.' They truly thought that was the best way to deal with the situation. But from that point on, Toby had a phobia not only of dogs, but of fur. He could not bear to touch furry toys or velvet. So the trigger of *one isolated aspect* of the trauma with the dog felt, to Toby, like a threatened repeat of the entire trauma. Until Toby received counselling he had not been able to make the connection between the original trauma and his phobia.

A symbolic phobia is where something really frightens a child because it carries some metaphorical reference to something frightening in their past.

In a symbolic, as opposed to an associative, phobia of dogs the child may not have had any trauma around *actual* dogs. 'Dog' is simply a metaphorical reference in his mind for *another* danger, which cannot be thought about or let into conscious awareness. 'Dog' may be a metaphor for the child's fear of his own rage, or wish to attack someone in his life; or it may be fear of the rage of his frightening parent, teacher, sibling, etc, whom he experienced as psychologically attacking him in some way – 'Biting my head off', for example.

continued

<table>
<tr><td align="center">TABLE 1: CONTINUED</td></tr>
</table>

Can it be both? Can a fear or phobia be associative and symbolic at the same time?

Yes. Here is an example.

Tony, aged ten

Tony was a very anxious boy. His life was blighted on a daily basis by fears of his Mummy dying. It was completely irrational. His mother was in her thirties, and very healthy. In therapy it became clear that his fear was both associative and symbolic. When he was three his father had died (leaving him with an associative phobia of parental death). But now his mother, who used to be full of life, was becoming more and more depressed, and more and more emotionally dead when with her children. Tony wept bitterly in therapy about how, when he lost his alive mother, it felt *as if* he had a 'dead' Mummy (symbolic fear). The metaphor of death was a replacement for his fear of his mother's loss of love for him.

So in symbolic phobias, as opposed to associative phobias, the *actual* object of fear is replaced by another one. For example, in order not to acknowledge to himself that his mother is frightening, the child may develop a phobia of spiders. The spider is actually a metaphor for his frightening mother. It is a system of self-denial: 'Mummy is fine. It's just spiders I don't like.' In other words, unbearable feelings can be diverted from the original focus to a new, and far less threatening, one. This means that the child will start to be afraid of *something entirely other than the thing about which he was originally afraid.* (See Figure 17)

Freud gave an example of this sort of replacement in the case of a little boy called 'Little Hans' he was treating (1979b). Little Hans was phobic of horses. Freud found that the boy had transformed his fear of his father in to a fear of horses. Having a phobia about horses meant that the little boy could still have a good relationship with his father and sustain his loving feelings for him *because all his frightening feelings were displaced on to horses.*

As Freud said about this child's phobia:

> One cannot get rid of a father; he can appear whenever he chooses. But if he is replaced by an animal, all one has to do is to

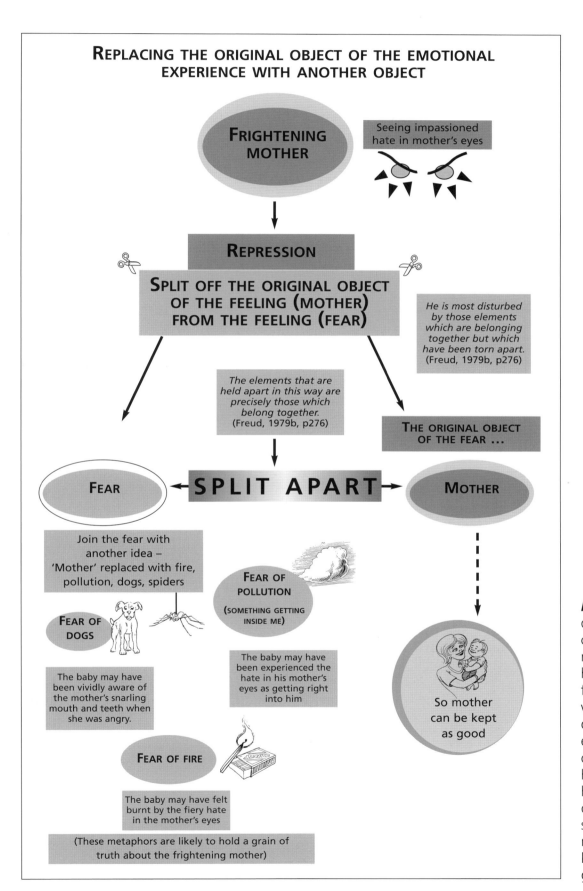

REPLACING THE ORIGINAL OBJECT OF THE EMOTIONAL EXPERIENCE WITH ANOTHER OBJECT

FRIGHTENING MOTHER

Seeing impassioned hate in mother's eyes

REPRESSION

SPLIT OFF THE ORIGINAL OBJECT OF THE FEELING (MOTHER) FROM THE FEELING (FEAR)

He is most disturbed by those elements which are belonging together but which have been torn apart. (Freud, 1979b, p276)

The elements that are held apart in this way are precisely those which belong together. (Freud, 1979b, p276)

THE ORIGINAL OBJECT OF THE FEAR ...

FEAR ← **SPLIT APART** → **MOTHER**

Join the fear with another idea – 'Mother' replaced with fire, pollution, dogs, spiders

FEAR OF POLLUTION

(SOMETHING GETTING INSIDE ME)

FEAR OF DOGS

The baby may have been vividly aware of the mother's snarling mouth and teeth when she was angry.

The baby may have been experienced the hate in his mother's eyes as getting right into him

FEAR OF FIRE

The baby may have felt burnt by the fiery hate in the mother's eyes

(These metaphors are likely to hold a grain of truth about the frightening mother)

So mother can be kept as good

Figure 17 As a defence, a child can replace, in his mind, the thing he is actually frightened of with something different. For example, instead of telling himself he is frightened of his mother, he can develop a fear of spiders. This means he can keep his mother good in his mind.

> avoid the sight of it – that is, its presence – in order to be free from danger and anxiety. 'Little Hans' therefore, imposed a restriction upon [himself]… He produced the inhibition of not leaving the house, so as not to come across any horses. (Freud, 1979b, p281)

It was this 'act of replacement' which meant that Freud could diagnose Little Hans as phobic.

> If 'Little Hans'… had shown fear of his father, we should have no right to say that he had a neurosis or a phobia. His emotional reaction would have been entirely comprehensible. What made it a neurosis was one thing alone: the replacement of his father by a horse. (Freud, 1979b, p256)

Take another example, a boy I worked with called Charlie. Charlie was 12. He replaced his fears of his mother's persistent emotional needs of him with a fear of encroaching spiders. Through counselling it became clear that Charlie experienced his single-parent mother as in some way 'getting right into' his mind through her misplaced, desperate emotional need for him as a kind of surrogate husband. His feelings about his mother were too unmanageable, so he had repressed them and ended up being terrified of spiders instead. Like so many children, Charlie needed his mother too much to do otherwise. He needed to see her as safe, not unsafe. It would have been too awful for Charlie to stay conscious of the fact that the very person he needed so much was *also* the one he feared. A spider was a good and accurate metaphor for his perception of his mother as coming at him from all directions – creepy and devouring its victim.

For Charlie, his spider phobia could seem a really smart way of dealing with his fears and anxiety, in that his neurotic symptom played an essential role in 'maintaining his sense of goodness about the world' (Armstrong-Permian, personal communication, 1994). It left him able to feel that 'My Mummy is lovely. It's just spiders I hate.' The trouble is that when a child uses neurotic symptoms to unconsciously bind fear and anxiety into a symptom like this, it usually spreads into a kind of all-pervading anxiety too. This happened with Charlie. He was never truly calm, never truly at rest.

Billy, aged seven

Billy had a symbolic phobia of thunderstorms; displaced from fears of his too 'emotionally loud', alcoholic father, who would come into the room with 'sudden crashes of shout' (as Billy described them when he trusted me enough). Once he had firmly located the thunderstorm back where it belonged, with his father, his phobia of them stopped.

Children's fears and phobias of fire

Charlie, aged seven

Charlie was the one child in his village who was in his house on bonfire night. He sat in his bedroom and shook. Ever since he had seen his father hit his mother, he had been frightened of fires.

As we have seen, because young children have not yet formed strong enough defence mechanisms, they cannot keep out stimuli as they would wish. Their world is dominated by strong sensations, and their brain is just too immature to defend against or moderate these through the power of thought. This means that children can be acutely sensitive to the intense, negative, or raw feelings of the grown-ups in their life. So it is not surprising that fire or flood or thunderstorm – that is, *a huge energy force that could so easily get out of control* – is often a focus of a child's obsession or phobia. Tragically, if untreated, a child can be left with this obsession or phobia for life.

All this raises a moral point about parents whose intense negative emotional states (whether anger or anxiety) repeatedly leak out or break out in the home, but who refuse therapeutic help for themselves. The awful intensity of their outbursts or leakages is so often due to their not having been given enough help with their own feelings in *their* childhood, and so not having established the stress-regulating mechanisms in their brains that were discussed earlier.

Furthermore, a parent's determination not to pass on to their child what they have suffered is sometimes in vain, as such determination is a *conscious* idea from the higher brain, and does not take into account the powerful leakage and hormonal forces triggered by the lower brain. We all know, in theory, that you do not dump your neurosis on your children, but if a parent's own childhood pain is too denied or unworked through, she will do just that, however hard she tries not to.

The tragedy is that parents who exude very frightening, 'fiery' feelings are often very passionate people. But because their childhood pain has been so denied or unworked through, their passion has 'gone wrong', so to speak. If they had sought help, or been given help at some time, to express and work through their childhood feelings, their passion could have been harnessed into something very creative, very positive. But when passion goes wrong – when it has grown too intense from too many years of bottling up – the child just receives the parental 'passion' in toxic form. The following poem illustrates how 'toxic passion' can be communicated to a child both verbally and in unspoken ways.

Cold Silences of a Mother
O venomous tool!
Such binge of hate to bring the air so stale,
To choke the play and light.
Your look, a silent shriek of blame
Its fumes now clinging to our skins,
Your little vicious gas
Cloaked in such sweet piety, *'Who me?'*

And so we skulk away like guilty dogs,
Whilst you so righteous there
Up high to see, to gloat our wounds
And how you've made us trap
Our words inside our mouths,
Your poisoned chill of mood and grudge,
Far worse than foul Medusa's eye.

Content? Off-loading years of bile
On your 'beloved ones' so-called
Who wander there within its fug;
Perfectly legal pollution, that eats away
With sores of shame at any conscience's flesh,
And brings about such wretched blight
Of fading into mute defeat.

Margot Sunderland

Colin, aged sixteen

Colin had been terrified all his young life of lights and all electrical appliances in his house catching fire. He made the following insightful comment in therapy: 'My mother couldn't help me with my own fire (passion), because she was so frightening, so full of bitterness and anger. So to me she was just more fire. I had to try to be the coolant for her. But my own fire had not actually gone out, it was just pushed underground, where I guess it became even more lethal and frightening. Now I see how I'm frightened of both my mother's fire and my own fire.' When Colin finally felt safe enough in therapy to fully feel and express 16 years of held-in fear, grief and rage, he no longer had an irrational fear of fire.

Children often portray the raw, unprocessed emotional intensity of a raging parent using images of fire in play

As we have seen, fire is a very accurate and powerful image for raw and primitive emotional intensity – an intensity that is being discharged instead of processed and thought through.

Sally, aged six

Sally's father was a wife-beater. He also hit Sally's two older brothers on many occasions, and often threatened Sally. It was unknown whether he had ever hit her. Sally's favourite song was *London's Burning*. In therapy she said :

☆ 'Dad keeps lighting fires.' (She is talking metaphorically.) 'In fact they are so big they become volcanoes. People keep falling in the volcanoes and getting burned.' (In other words, she may have felt that the people in her family kept getting metaphorically burnt – scarred by her father's terrible raging.)

☆ 'Mummy and two baby pigs get burned and don't get found. My brother is trying to climb over a mountain of fire, but he doesn't make it.' (A feeling, perhaps, that her siblings did not psychologically survive the father's rage.)

☆ 'On the street, people tell me that my Daddy is dead.'(Wishful thinking?)

☆ 'I'm going to play something scary now at the bottom of the piano.'

Children's phobias are fuelled by a fear of their own too-strong feelings

> There is such a thing as living in constant expectation of disaster coming from within. (Herman, 1988, p122)

When children have not been helped enough with their intense feelings of rage, fear or separation distress, they can also develop a phobia or obsession. This time the displaced fears are of the child's own raw, emotional intensity. In such cases his fear of himself and his too-powerful feelings, which are experienced as far too dangerous, must be replaced with a fear of something *outside* himself.

Tommy, aged six

Tommy was phobic about walking on busy streets. He was certain that a double-decker bus would suddenly lose control, swerve on to the pavement and kill him or his Mummy. Tommy had learnt all too early that his rage was dangerous because, from the age of two, whenever he had a temper tantrum his mother threatened to send him away if he did not stop it at once. So Tommy did not get angry any more. The problem was that his anger did not just disappear, he simply repressed it. But as Freud said, repressed feelings banished to the unconscious simply 'proliferate in the dark' (1979a, p148). So Tommy's destructive impulses were displaced on to a dread of double-decker buses coming towards him.

In therapy, Tommy was able to get in touch once more with his feelings of rage. As a result, week after week, he joyfully drove toy double-decker buses in a sandpit over a character he called Mrs Pudding (probably his mother, Figure 18). He would laugh and laugh with relief as his raging impulses, which were squashed in the two-year-old Tommy, were now both witnessed and accepted by an adult. His therapist, unlike his mother, enabled him to realize that his

Figure 18 Tommy drove toy double-decker buses in a sandpit over a character he called Mrs Pudding. At last he was able to integrate his feelings of rage after years of being a very frightened little boy.

feelings were natural and understandable, rather than dangerous. His therapist helped Tommy to process his rage through thinking and verbal expression. As a result, Tommy no longer needed to either repress his rage or discharge it.

This example of phobic defence is very understandable. If a child replaces a fear of *himself* with a fear of something *outside himself*, he can simply avoid that thing or event – for example, he can stay away from spiders, double-decker buses or vicious dogs. But if he lets himself know that what *really* feels frightening and 'attacking' are his *own* feelings – which in Tommy's case he believes are so dangerous they could cause his mother to abandon him – then he is helpless and powerless because the danger *is him*. Children can keep on running from themselves endlessly in this way. But, of course, locating the danger outside himself takes a child ever further from getting help with the fear of his own feelings, and finding adults who can both normalise and understand them.

> In phobias it is very easy to observe the way in which this internal danger is transformed into an external one – that is to say, how a neurotic anxiety is changed into an apparently realistic one. (Freud, 1979c, p116)

> External dangers are experienced in the light of internal dangers and are therefore intensified. (Klein, 1975a, p32)

Tony, aged eight

Tony catastrophised about being killed by bombs secretly planted somewhere in his bedroom or garden, or in the park where he played. He was sometimes so distressed at bedtime that his parents would make up a little bed for him in the lounge. (For some reason, Tony believed the bad men would not plant bombs in the lounge.)

In counselling, Tony was encouraged to get in touch with his own aggression – starting with a marshmallow fight with his counsellor – and he realised that he felt like a bomb! He then endlessly enacted dropping bombs on the heads of peanut people in the sandtray. He became confident and assertive. Therapy helped him, not only to no longer be frightened of his own anger, but also to find words for it. 'I am very angry today,' he would come in and say confidently.

Tony was lucky. He was enabled to understand his terrifying 'bomb' metaphor. For many fearful children, who are not fortunate enough to be given counselling or therapy, such a defence mechanism holds too high a price. This is because locating the danger as something *outside* yourself means that you then often perceive the *outer* world as very frightening and dangerous. In other words, the outer world is then experienced against the terrifying backdrop of your too-threatening inner world. Life is still lived with a feeling of threat. The *danger is just outside rather than inside*.

> One can save oneself from an external danger by flight; fleeing from an internal danger is a difficult enterprise. (Freud, 1979c, p117)

Children's fears and phobias of monsters and animals with teeth as images of their own disowned aggression

Some childrens' fears or phobias of sharks, dogs, etc, can once again be their own disowned aggression. This is often the case in children whose natural rage and anger met with heavy disapproval from parents. The child then moved into compliance and 'being good'. Anything less might have meant a catastrophic loss of his parents' love and approval. Disowned anger builds up pressure in the child's unconscious, while haunting his conscious mind with something very dangerous and attacking. This is then projected on to some other 'aggressive creature', which is feared. This is partly why films like *Jaws* are so successful – some people identify with the frightened folk on the beach, some with the sharks! They would love to bite off someone's head! It is just not safe for them to let the reality of their own aggressive impulses enter their awareness.

I am constantly amazed at the number of children in sandplay therapy (a therapy using miniature images and objects, placed in a box of sand in order to symbolise one's inner world and dreamlife) who have an aversion at the beginning of the session to one or more of the toy monsters in the room – sharks, or animals with teeth. But at the end of the session, they sit looking fondly at that same shark or monster, or even sit there hugging it! They have re-owned a split-off, or previously disowned and deeply-buried, part of themselves. They have been able to accept the fact that they have angry attacking feelings too.

The terror when 'I feel stronger than my Mummy'

In times of outright defiance, children can experience themselves as stronger than their parent. This can make them feel very powerful, but at the same time very frightened. Such children often have nightmares of monsters, which can also come out repeatedly in their play. Sometimes they develop phobias. These stop when the therapist helps the parent to manage the child's anger and defiant behaviour effectively, so the child will not feel like a powerful monster. I have seen this played out many times in my parent–child work when a child is brought to therapy as 'out-of-control'. When I ask both parent and child to pick a miniature toy to represent themselves, the 'out-of-control' child always picks some kind of monster, and the parent a very powerless thing – a lamb or little child, etc. Well, there is the problem!

Gemma, aged five

Gemma was brought into therapy by her mother for being uncontrollable at times, particularly in the morning before going to school. Typically, the little girl was terrified of monsters, had lots of nightmares and a phobia of dogs. When asked what she would like most from her mother, the little girl said, *'I want you to help me with my monsters.'* She was referring to her own raging feelings. After the mother was helped to find ways of controlling her child the little girl stopped having nightmares, and was far better behaved because she now had a mother who had indeed helped her with her monsters.

Understanding obsessions and compulsive rituals in children

A compulsive ritual is where a child tries to handle their worry and anxiety through *action*. This is the opposite of a phobia, where the child deals with their worry and anxiety by *avoidance*.

Compulsive behaviour or ritual is something done time and time again in order to ward off an imagined dreaded event in the mind – an event that feels all too real. This is why it is often called obsessive-compulsive behaviour, not just compulsive behaviour, because the child obsessively imagines or thinks about something awful happening, which he is then convinced will happen unless he carries out his compulsive ritual. The child feels 'out-of-control' and impotent in dealing with a threatening feeling and thought, so the compulsive action helps him to feel in control.

Compulsive rituals are a defence against anxiety – the anxiety of an emotional intensity which the child cannot manage any other way. The anxiety is a neurotic defence against feeling, one or more of the following emotions, which are experienced as far too dangerous:

1   Fear
2   Rage
3   Grief (fear of loss, actual loss, or denied grieving).

The child is unable to deal with his anxiety through thinking, feeling or talking about it, so he deals with the angst through action. The ritual is then a way he makes himself feel safer in the world and the world a less frightening place in which to be. The ritual is used to fend off some perceived danger. (There may be no actual danger in his outer world, but there is in his imagination.) Furthermore, usually subconsciously, the child often fears losing control in some way – that his rage, fear or grief will just spill out in some awful, intense mess, destroying himself and/or his loved ones.

When humans are stressed they opt either for comfort from others or control. Children who have given up on adults as a source of comfort (or never known this in the first place) are very likely to opt for control.

Compulsive rituals leave the realm of common sense. So, although the child has already checked eight times that there is no monster under the bed, the obsessive fear of the awful event in his mind (if there *was* a monster under the bed) is so great, and feels so real, that he must carry out the ritual, *'in case...*
in case'.

In compulsive rituals, a child assesses the actual likelihood of danger wrongly. What is very very *unlikely* feels very very *likely*. Even the remotest possibility of an imagined catastrophe feels to the child like a near certainty, *because he has seen it so vividly in his mind*.

> ... even the tiniest percent of a chance of a disaster means that disaster is inevitable. (Dumont, 1996, p268)

> Magic thinkers feel they need 100 percent certainty, while the rest of us fumble along on faith and hope. (Dumont, 1996, p237)

It is never OK to coerce a child into stopping a ritual. In his mind carrying it out feels like a matter of life or death. A compulsive ritual is not something the child can just stop. Will-power is useless.

Common examples of compulsive rituals in children

☆ Repeatedly checking they have done something, when they have already done it

☆ Repeatedly washing their hands, when they have already washed them

☆ Repeatedly flushing the toilet (once is not enough)

☆ Repeatedly cleaning something

☆ Repeatedly touching something

Such rituals are often extremely time-consuming.

If a child suffers from compulsive rituals his *inner* world of feelings, thoughts and images is a terrifyingly unpredictable place – where, for example, fires could start any minute, or lethal germs could kill – no matter how safe his *outer* world is in reality. His inner world houses images of terrifying events, often of mythological proportions, including death, fire, flood, accidents or the end of the world. In his mind he sees the imagined burning, the death, the terrible explosion, the devastation of all that is safe and 'good' in his life. Hence the desperation in the child completing his ritual when he believes this action will prevent his nightmare from happening.

Emma, aged six

Emma went into psychotherapy for her compulsive washing rituals and night terrors. In therapy, she kept washing her doll's face. She said it was so grubby, she couldn't get it clean. She was distraught because she said there was only grubby water to wash the dirty face with, when in fact the water was quite clean. It seemed that in her imagination at that moment, *everything* felt unclean or polluted, not just her doll!

It later became clear that she felt contaminated by images of her mother's face, which would distort with rage if Emma was naughty in any way. It was clear these images had got under her skin. As she talked in therapy about being very, very scared of her mother's eyes when her mother was cross, it was clear that in this desperate episode with the doll she was trying to wash away the terrifying expressions she had seen too often on her mother's face.

Emma's experience is common: many children and adults obsessively wash themselves or something else, in order (subconsciously), to literally try to get rid of terrifying images from their past that have been imprinted too vividly in to their memory.

How to recognise the difference between a developmentally natural ritual and a concerning one

It is quite natural for young children to move into some form of compulsive ritual and repetitive behaviour – for example, an urgent and pressing need to do something or to avoid doing something, to touch something or to avoid touching something or a compulsion to count or list.

Typically a child might say 'I mustn't step on the crack' or 'I must touch the railings each time I go past.' There is an underlying sense of 'If I do not do this, something awful will happen.' This is often referred to as 'magical thinking'. The ritual is therefore used to fend off some perceived danger. (There may be no actual danger in his outer world, but there is in his imagination.)

Magical thinking in young children is very common, as their imagination is developing apace, while their grasp of reality may still be fragile. We know this because children from two to six years old often state something totally imagined as if it were reality. For example, Billy's father asked Billy, aged three, if he had seen the car keys. Billy said he had buried them in the gravel. He had not, but his father spent over an hour looking in the gravel. Nathan, aged five, who had just arrived in Spain after getting off the aeroplane, looked up at another aeroplane in the sky and said in a very matter-of-fact voice, 'That aeroplane is bringing my toys to Spain for me. It's a special toy plane.'

Things can often get worse at the age of four – often referred to as 'the fearful fours' – a time when the child's imagination is really taking off (hence often superbly imaginative play), but so is his conscious awareness of his fear.

However, children tend to grow out of magical thinking, although we still see its remnants in adult superstition – for example, 'Don't walk under ladders' or 'Don't say "Macbeth" before the play.' But if a child continues to show obsessional behaviours well into later primary school years, and the behaviours persist for over six months, getting more intense rather than less, then it is a good time to intervene and get help.

Childhood obsessions and compulsive rituals that can be concerning may happen after children suffer a significant life change – such as going to a new school; the birth of a sibling; a parental separation; or when they have suffered a trauma such as bereavement. As we have seen, fear, rage or grief as a result of the life change are experienced as too dangerous by the child to let into conscious awareness. The child is not able to deal with this 'dangerous' feeling through thinking about it or fully feeling it or talking about it, so he deals with it through *action*.

A child suffering from obsessions or compulsive rituals that last over six months or so needs help with his feelings, as the ritual or obsession shows that he is 'self-holding'. This means trying to manage his feelings all by himself, without asking for help from the grown-ups in his life. 'Self-holding' never works for a child, in the sense that there is always neurotic fallout. In contrast, children who firmly believe in the value of 'help' from grown-ups (because in the past it has really helped them to tell a grown-up what is troubling them) will be far less likely to resort to obsessions and rituals to handle their feelings. In short, the child either gets soothing from a grown-up for his distress and his fear, or turns to the soothing he can get out of performing his ritual. When the obsessive child performs his ritual – for example, flushing the toilet eight times, or pulling his socks on and off repeatedly in the morning – it makes him feel more emotionally together, calmer. Hence, if an adult comes along and tries to interrupt his ritual, he can feel very distressed indeed.

If a child shows persistent obsessional behaviours it in no way points to bad parenting. However, it may be that a parent is struggling with unprocessed feelings left over from her *own* childhood, or some undigested trauma or loss from later life. If a parent is defending against her own unbearable feelings, then she can be what is known as 'mind-blind' to the intense feelings her child is having. Action in the form of ritual obsession is therefore a child's form of self-help. Children sense, on a very deep unconscious level, if a parent is emotionally unavailable and unable to help them with their feelings.

Sophie, aged six

Sophie was defending against unbearable grief from having lost her Daddy who had left to live with another woman abroad. After her father had left, Sophie developed a compulsive ritual. She needed to touch all the railings on the way to and from school. She would do this by putting her hand in her pocket, and did it so much that a huge hole appeared in her coat. Sophie's mother was well-meaning, but defending against her own grief about her husband leaving, so she was unable to help Sophie with any of her feelings of loss.

In order to try to help a child curb his habit of self-help through compulsive ritual, he must be enabled to manage his feelings another way – ideally through getting empathic help from a grown-up. If a child is not convinced that sharing his feelings with a parent will soothe distress, he may stick firmly to rituals to manage his 'dangerous' feelings. When this happens, sometimes the best action for the parent is to seek outside help.

Understanding why a fearful child can develop physical symptoms

I once worked with a little boy called Simon, whose father developed a drink problem when Simon was around six years old. His father would arrive home drunk, and shouting and raging. At seven years old the little boy had developed asthma and eczema, was prone to colds, and would sick up water several times a day in the classroom. In effect, his body was exploding as a result of his exploding father. No-one had given Simon any help with his relational stress, so all he could do was to move into a primitive discharge of unbearable emotional and physical arousal, caused by his intense level of fear.

For some children, their fear interferes with natural bodily processes like sleeping, defecating and eating. Some cannot take in food and develop eating disorders.

Everything he took inside seemed to him bad, damaged and poisonous ... so there was no point eating anything' (Rosenfeld, 1965, p81)

Sleeping may be far too dangerous. To sleep, there must be a skeletal surrender. This is antipathetical for a child who feels with all his body and mind that he must be hyper-vigilant.

> The full terror of the experience of the world is liable at any moment to crash in and obliterate all identity as a gas will rush in and obliterate a vacuum. (Laing, 1990, p45)

From anxious parent to anxious child

A child with too much daily contact with a parent figure who is too often anxious or on edge, can all too easily develop a picture of the world as a very unsafe, unpredictable place. (This is particularly the case where there has been no other calming central parent-figure to dilute or compensate for the anxious energy.)

A child can build up a picture of the world as being *like* their anxious parent – a place where something worrying or even catastrophic could happen at any time. In short, the child generalises from the parent to the world.

Margaret, aged ten

Margaret's mother had numerous phobias. Margaret similarly suffered from a phobia of enclosed spaces. The story she enacted in therapy was about a jangled, tangled mess. In a moment of insight she said, 'But I keep getting tangled up in my Mummy's tangled mess too.'

Julia, aged four

Julia had problems sleeping. She told the teacher that water kept coming through her ceiling at night. (She was speaking metaphorically. Children aged four and under often speak about something metaphorical as if it was reality.) She was worried that the ceiling would cave in. During therapy it became clear that this was actually a metaphor for her fears that her mother – the person on whom she depended to be strong and safe – might collapse emotionally at any moment. Who would look after her then? Her mother told the counsellor that she did indeed often feel on the edge of a breakdown. When Julia's mother got help, Julia's anxieties about the ceiling vanished.

Sally, aged twelve

Sally was terrified of underground trains. She said it was the thought of 'all those people panicking', if something should go wrong. Sally's mother was extremely anxious, and Sally had been repeatedly and profoundly impacted by the look of anxiety that was a regular feature on her mother's face. In therapy, for the first time, Sally started to be calm. Her therapist helped her to see that she had been re-traumatising herself each time she went on public transport by searching for the anxious faces, rather than the calm ones. The next time she went on the train, she sought out the calm faces and felt fine.

To a child, his mother *is* his world. A mother's highly anxious state can be perceived very intensely by a young undefended child, as if it was multiplied, and all over everything – hence Sally's fear of 'all those people panicking'. By and large, anxious parents are parents who have not had enough help with their own fear and anxieties when they were children. They are not in any way bad parents, simply unhelped parents – often doing their very best, but carrying a legacy of anxiety and fear from their own childhood. When not addressed in themselves, their fears and anxieties can all too easily be passed down generationally.

Whether they like it or not, parents are powerful role models for fear and anxiety. Below are 'frightened' statements, which neurotically anxious parents often convey to their children, either verbally or non-verbally.

☆ Authority figures are to be frightened of.

☆ If you do something wrong, you will feel terrible.

☆ Do not ever really relax, because that is when things go wrong.

☆ Be safe, not sorry.

☆ Try to be perfect, because mistakes are awful things.

☆ Taking risks, or being spontaneous, will only lead to something bad.

☆ It is a terrible thing not to have security, money, a partner, a home, a job etc, so stick to them like glue.

☆ Never get into debt.

Children often have the very same fears or phobias as their parents – sometimes, tragically, in a more extreme form. Metaphorically speaking, the child gets all muddled up in his parents' anxieties until they become *his* anxieties. Here is some of the key research:

> In a study of 70 pre-school children aged from two to six years and their mothers, Hagman (1932) found significant correlation between the children who feared dogs and the mothers who feared dogs, and also between children and mothers who feared insects. A correlation was also present, though of lower degree, between children and mothers who feared thunderstorms. (Bowlby, 1973, p160)

> About one-sixth of adults with fears have a close relative with a similar phobia. (Marks, 1971, p683)

A main focus for some parents' neurotic anxiety and catastrophising can be the child himself. The parent fears that the child will die or get injured in some awful way. Most parents fear this on some level; but it is the persistency and intensity of their fear which reveals neurotic anxiety. For some children, the effect of being such a central focus for their parents' fear (even when unstated) can be that, again, they see the world as a very frightening, unsafe place where something awful could happen at any moment.

Balint, a psychoanalyst, makes the point well:

> Instead of live infants, they were seen, perhaps, as frightening objects who might easily die, and so they experienced their mothers and the world in which they were living as full of dread and fear. (1993, p108)

Looked at from another angle, if a parent is too stressed and anxious for too much of the time, she simply does not have enough 'mental or emotional space' to be able to truly soothe her child, to quell his fire of anxiety or agitation. She is too busy trying to manage her own! If the child does not have regular daily access to a *non-anxious* other adult, he will not experience that essential merging again and again of his anxious body-mind with a calm, strong body-presence, into which he can truly let go and experience a deep state of peace. This is *vital* if a child is to know real inner peace as an adult.

Some children are deeply affected by parental agitation and tension that pervades the family home like some terrible fog. A child may start to associate his mother with this anxious, agitated, unregulated energy and so begin to find ways to protect himself from it. It may result in a troubled, uncomfortable or too distant relationship between parent and child. (Some psychologists believe that some children on the autistic spectrum, with no neurological damage, show autistic behaviour because they have already switched off from their mother's too jarring, dysregulating voice in the womb.)

Peter, aged ten

Peter in therapy made the two pictures on page 69. He felt overwhelmed, in a chaotic world. His mother and father were agitated and anxious people. Both were constantly needing to get things right as a manic defence against shame (a legacy from their own childhoods). In front of Peter, both would regularly voice their worries about money; the house; Peter's physical health; what the neighbours were thinking; the security of their front door; the gas bill, and so on. Peter was overwhelmed by the raw, primitive fearful discharge of both parents. The pictures he painted express this so clearly.

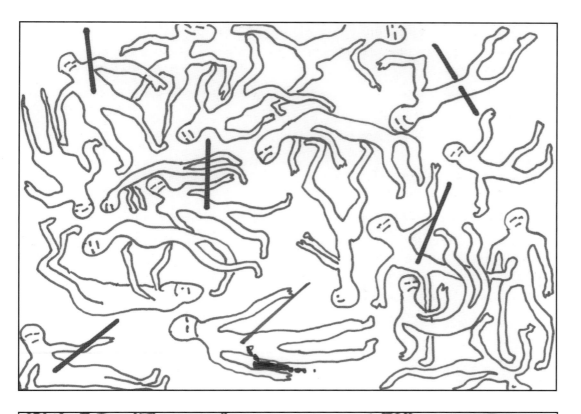

Figure 19 Peter, aged 10, felt overwhelmed in a chaotic world. His mother and father were very anxious on a regular basis. He spoke very eloquently about his inner world through these images.

From needy parent to fearful child

> My mother is the moon; she is a huge funnel. She is chasing me across a great empty space to suck me in; I run and run, faster, faster, but always she is just behind me. I come to the edge of the world and jump off. I am falling down, down into darkness. While I am falling, I wake in terror. (Wickes, 1976, pp111–12)

Such frightening images of the over-close or needy parent are typical of children who have been afraid of being engulfed, taken over, or merged in their relationship with a parent. Yet, unlike in the dream above, many children with these fears split them off from their source, the parent. This means they can leave their positive feelings for their parent intact. 'It is just spiders, or strangers getting too physically close, and so on, that I'm frightened of.' The feelings of invasion, being engulfed or emotionally suffocated are displaced on to all manner of other objects or people.

Some children with emotionally needy parents, may develop physical symptoms. Segal reports how adult asthma-sufferers often complain in psychotherapy of having felt emotionally suffocated by their mothers as children (1985, p30). Their breathing difficulties can be a way of expressing feelings of *inability to breathe* because their mother is *all around them*. Some children fear, on a symbolic level, that the mother is so threateningly close that she could be 'breathed right in'. Thus they are expressing through metaphor the fear of losing all sense of self in the face of an overpowering other. 'The fundamental terror is "being swallowed up in the other's personality"' (Guntrip, 1969).

Some children grow up fearing intimacy because they have felt themselves to be the focus of intense parental need. The parent may have needed the child to adore her; to listen to all *her* problems or to be a substitute partner in some way. Or a parent may overwhelm the child with her own worries, anxieties or other complex adult feelings. Or the child may feel that he is in some sense drowning in the swamps of his mother's depression, which she chooses to speak about with *him*, as opposed to with another adult. So many needy parents tragically leak out their own unmet childhood need for love and attention, which now becomes the burden of their own child.

Children with a needy, depressed or mentally ill parent often do their very best to answer the needs of that parent, while simultaneously feeling overwhelmed, helpless, impotent and desperately inadequate. Such children can grow up equating intimacy with something threatening. Intimacy can too easily re-trigger feelings of impotence, fear and failure – the very feelings they had around their parents' needs. They can be left with a chronic fear that anyone who gets close or loves them will demand more from them than they can give. Or they may fear that the needs of the other will threaten their very sense of self, suck them dry, or take from them in ways they cannot afford to give. This can send them into a debilitating emotional paralysis, reliving the impossibility they felt of ever meeting the needs of their parent.

Tessa

From childhood, Tessa had suffered acute claustrophobia. Her proud mother said to her adult daughter, who had grown up feeling terrified of intimacy, 'I never left you alone for a moment as a child.' Tessa's feeling of being constantly watched over, monitored, touched, admired, drooled over and smothered with love, had left her with years of feeling suffocated, frightened and trapped.

Alice did not much like keeping so close to her: first because the Duchess was very ugly; and secondly because she was exactly the right height to rest her chin upon Alice's shoulder, and it was an uncomfortably sharp chin. (Carroll, 1994, p95)

THINGS TO SAY AND WAYS TO BE WITH FEARFUL CHILDREN

For many children who are frightened, the first step is to *help them to voice their fear*. (The practical exercises in the next chapter can really help here.) As we have seen, many fearful children have never actually talked to anyone about feeling frightened. Instead, it has just become a way of life to deal all alone with the things that frighten them. Many have no idea that they can get help with what scares them, and because they have never asked for help, they remain just as frightened as ever.

So many fearful children have absolutely no notion of what a life free of fear would be like. They think that feeling frightened every day is just a part of life; something you have to endure. And yet, on a day-to-day basis, their fear is spoiling their life, depriving them of that lovely feeling of being at ease and at peace in a warm world.

The fearful child usually gives himself one option in the face of a frightening relationship – to react rather than act. He simply hangs around and waits for the other person to have a feeling, to which he will then react. Expressing his own feelings, or even acknowledging that he has any, is usually not part of his repertoire. This resigned impotence is often fuelled by a belief in one or more of the following:

☆ It is not safe for me to have any feelings here.

☆ There is no space for my feelings as well as theirs.

☆ I do not even let myself know I am frightened.

So before the fearful child is able to take action, he often needs time to reflect on what is frightening him, to stop denying, deflecting from or desensitising around his fear. We hope that the next two chapters will enable you to offer the fearful child just that: an extremely rich and safe reflection time from which he can feel both deeply understood and empowered.

Useful things to say, and important psychological messages for children with a fearful attitude to life

☆ It is a very brave thing to tell a kind grown-up that something is frightening you. It means that you have the courage to speak out, rather than just keeping the frightening things all bottled up inside you.

☆ Did you know that all children have rights, just like adults? Rights to be respected and treated well. In fact, the UK government has a very long book all about the rights of children. It is a book called *The Children's Act* (Stationery Office, 1989). A lot of grown-ups wrote it to try to make sure that children are treated well. The book says it is against the law for a child to be treated badly. So you have what are called human rights – rights not to be hit, hurt or frightened by an adult.

☆ It makes all the difference in the world if you are doing something that feels frightening, or too difficult, together with someone else, instead of all on your own. Try to always get some 'togetherness'. (You may want to read the child the story *Teenie Weenie in a Too Big World* – Sunderland, 2003 – as it is all about the awfulness of aloneness and the loveliness of togetherness, in the face of fear.)

☆ 'Feel the fear and do it anyway!' (Jeffers, 1987) – as long as it is something that will be good for you, rather than harmful or hurtful to you in any way. If you are not sure about this, check it out with a kind grown-up. Remember, you can always, 'feel the fear and do it anyway, with someone else helping you!'

☆ Did you know that the really, really frightening things in life usually involve you feeling all alone with *someone* who is frightening rather than *something* that is frightening? Natural things like thunderstorms, or very strong winds or the dark, can feel far less scarey than scarey people, because you can find someone to be with you when these things happen.

☆ Some grown-ups just do not know they are frightening children unless someone tells them. Some of them, the OK ones, will be very sad and thoughtful if someone tells them they are frightening children, and they will stop doing it. Sometimes you need to ask a kind grown-up to speak to a frightening grown-up. This is not cowardly, it is really sensible and clever.

☆ Grown-ups who frighten children a lot usually do it because another grown-up frightened them when they were a child! You might say to them something like, 'I am sorry you had an unhappy childhood.' This can make them think about what you are saying, rather than just keeping on frightening children the way they were frightened.

☆ The best way of dealing with grown-ups who frighten you with their words or faces is to say what you feel and what you need. 'Excuse me but you are frightening me, so I can't really listen to what you are saying. Please speak to me with a quieter voice.' It is really cool to do this particularly if a kind grown-up is there with you as you say it.

☆ If the frightening grown-up is too much like a mad volcano and so you are worried that they might erupt, then go to a kind adult and say what you feel. For example: *'My teacher is frightening me. Can you do something about it?'* In clearly stating your needs like this, you can move from being a frightened child into being a child with rights. A child who knows his rights is a great child to be.

☆ When children make mistakes they need to be treated with kindness, not with crossness. If children meet crossness when they make a mistake, it can make them frightened of making mistakes, which is a very sad thing.

☆ 'A big person is not someone who never falls down. A big person is someone who, when they fall, does what it takes to get up again.' (Williamson, 1992, p171).

Helping the fearful child to find his 'no'

> Until [a child] has a strong NO in his repertoire, he cannot have a strong YES. When he has a strong No ... he is safe ... and therefore he can also say Yes. (Resnick, personal communication, 1993)

As previously stated, fearful children often do not know they have human rights. They make themselves feel safe by running away or avoiding, as opposed to asserting their rights. So helping fearful children with how to be assertive, and with how to say 'NO' and 'STOP', is vital in helping them to move from a feeling of impotence (the major fuel of fear) to empowerment. As Sue Reid, a child psychotherapist, says:

> The child who hasn't really learnt the power of 'no' and experimented with it fully hasn't yet discovered his or her sense of self. It is as important to say 'no' as it is to be told 'no'. (1992, p19)

Helping fearful children to assert themselves

> A person who knows, perhaps without ever having thought about it – that if the situation demands it he can ... defend himself, is and feels strong. A person who registers the fact that he probably cannot do this is and feels weak. (Horney, 1977, p251)

Children need help to know that self-assertion does not mean aggression. They need to know that assertion means standing up for yourself, and putting down clear boundaries without putting down the other person. When one's basic human right to be treated with respect is being affronted, the capacity to move into natural assertiveness, as opposed to raw instinctual rage, is an essential tool. It is vital for getting things done in life, for getting people to listen to you, for being really clear with others about what you want and do not want, and what you will not put up with. Without this natural assertiveness children and adults alike are weakened, diminished, and in danger of being used or abused. (In the next section of the book you will find several exercises to help a fearful child with assertiveness skills.)

Some key steps towards self-assertive interaction, outlined in terms of rational-emotive therapy

1   Get the person's attention.

2   Describe, objectively, the other person's behaviour that you have difficulty with.

3   Communicate your healthy negative feelings.

4 Check your interpretations, and invite a response.

5 Listen to the other's response and give feedback.

6 State your preferences clearly and specifically.

7 Request agreement from the other person.

(Dryden & Gordon, 1994, pp117–9)

Emma, aged ten	**Version for a Child**
1 Get the person's attention	'Mummy, can I speak to you a minute?'
2 Say: 'When you…'	'When you shout at me…'
3 'I feel…'	'I feel frightened.'
4 'So what I want is…'	'So what I want is that you tell me in a quieter voice when I am doing something you really dislike.'
5 'Will you…?'	'Will you do it?'

You can role-play this with a child, using a real-life frightening situation that is bothering him.

Fearful children are usually fearful because, in some fundamental way, they are just not being clear and assertive. They are not saying clearly what they want and do not want, and how they feel about the way they are being treated. All fearful children need help with this. Often it has never occurred to them that they could protest to the frightening grown-up – or, if that is too frightening or dangerous, that they could protest to another grown-up (a kind one) about the frightening one. So helping the fearful child with basic assertiveness skills is empowering him.

Remember to discuss with the child if they need a kind grown-up by their side while they state their protest to a frightening grown-up. Never make the fearful child climb Everest. The fearful child is a child who has always known too much aloneness and needs to experience the wonders of human support and togetherness.

Fear is experienced viscerally, so a fearful child needs help to feel empowered in his body

Fearful children often have an image of their body as just too weak, too vulnerable, too open. Therefore, to enable frightened children to feel physically empowered through such things as martial arts or voice-work can be hugely effective in moving them on from fear to assertiveness. Both these particular interventions will them help experience themselves as stronger, and as taking up more space, psychologically speaking.

It is not possible to feel intense fear and intense anger at the same time. They are different circuits in the subcortex of the brain. So helping a child to get in touch with his assertiveness – his 'No' – on a physical level, is a vital step in enabling him to feel empowered enough to find his natural sense of 'protest'. Also give the child simple breathing exercises. Ask him to take the time in fearful situations to take some deep breaths, to ground himself by being aware of his stance, distributing weight equally on both feet, back straight, shoulders down. The body will then give a different message to the brain. It can dramatically reduce the impulse to run away or to cower or hide.

How to be with grown-ups who hit

Many children know that it is wrong for a grown-up to hit a child, but it can help them if you find the words for why:

'No grown-up should hit a child. It means they are not respecting your rights as a child. Your body is very precious, and should never be hurt like this. But there are some people in life who hurt children, who you should never tackle on your own. These are people who if you are really brave and say "STOP" or "NO" or "ENOUGH", it can make them even more angry, and they could hurt you even more. Always get help with these people. Tell a kind grown-up about what is happening, and then get their help. You really need some "togetherness" with this one.'

'Some grown-ups do bad things to children, then they say, "If you tell what I have done to you, I will do something awful to you." Often this is a very cruel trick, and they would not do these things. If someone is doing this cruel trick to you, you are far too alone, and so you need some togetherness. So tell a kind grown-up, about both the cruel trick and what the person is doing to you. This next wise saying might help you:

> Sometimes life hands you situations when all you can do is put one foot in front of the other and live moment to moment.' (Brown, 1991, p149)

Why being angry is often uncharted territory for fearful children — so they will often need some persuading!

> If the outside world is felt to be hostile, if one feels helpless toward it, then taking any risk of annoying people seems sheer recklessness. (Horney, 1977, p252)

If a child experiences an adult as a frightening monster, usually the last thing he wants to do is to upset that monster by being assertive or angry, because of the risk that the monster may get even angrier. So the fearful child often just moves into trying to please the grown-up who is frightening him. This makes him feel even weaker, and the giant still stronger. Moreover, the child's compliance rarely works to stop all outbursts from the adult with too much unprocessed rage left over from their *own* childhood. Such adults do not suddenly become well-behaved because they have an over-compliant child. It can sometimes make things worse, as the grown-up smells weakness and attacks it.

But to the fearful child faced with a frightening adult, it can feel as if anything less than total compliance would be risking far too much. This is particularly likely for a child who at some time has dared to stand up to a parent or teacher who has then exploded – leaving the child feeling, 'Well, I won't try *that* again!' Also, expressing anger to a frightening parent may evoke the fear of losing the love of that parent – a love the child may feel very insecure about. He learns instead to be a good child, and a good child in his mind means one without any angry feelings.

So, empowering a child to move from fear to assertion or anger can be a difficult step. He may feel very frightened that his anger will just cause more mess, or trigger more 'volcanoes'. As Orbach says of one of her patients who had just found her anger:

> Recognising her anger didn't just make her feel visible, it made her feel enormous and ungainly as though she was taking up much more space than she ought' (1994, p59).

It can be like this with fearful children. So one must be very careful not to push a child to move from fear into anger without due respect for the feelings of dread this may evoke.

Furthermore, as we have seen some children take a frightened position in life, *because they are frightened of their own anger as well as that of others.* For the fearful child, anger has often been modelled by a teacher or parent as something very horrible, out of control and dangerous. So the child will not suddenly think that anger is useful. There may also have been an occasion when the fearful child did get angry, but it resulted in something catastrophic for him. Perhaps a parent erupted even more, withdrew into a cold silence or broke down in tears. Therefore, with the fearful child, you will often need to explore what he feels is frightening about expressing anger. It is a good idea to get the child to draw what he imagines would happen if he got angry.

Some fearful children may have no idea that they bear any angry feelings towards a grown-up who has frightened them. Needless to say, all children who have been persistently frightened by an insensitive, raging or over-controlling adult *will* feel anger – it is just that they may well have suppressed or repressed it, because it felt too dangerous to do anything else. And yet without being able to feel anger, let alone express it, children will inevitably be left to live their lives feeling defenceless and fearful. They are living life without a vital resource. This is because anger (expressed from a thinking place rather than just a place of primitive discharge) is a boundary-setting emotion. It tells the other person exactly what you want, do not want and will not put up with.

The following are both fearful children with catastrophic beliefs about their own anger:

> **Jamie, aged six**
> Jamie's father often erupted in anger. Jamie said, 'Oh, I can't be angry, because if I shout, my voice will break all the windows.'

> **Sean, aged ten**
> In the early stages of counselling, Sean said, 'I have to be Nice Sean because Beastly Sean would scream so loud there would be a thunderstorm. I'm very frightened of thunderstorms.' However, after several months, Sean began to feel his anger towards his cruel step-mother whom he had feared for many years: 'When the witch was dead and in her coffin, one of the little people still bashed her up, and bashed her up and bashed her up. They didn't want to stop.'

There can be a very strong force of anger indeed when a fearful child who has repressed all his angry feelings starts to give up his defences.

Helping fearful children to realise that their feelings are as important as the feelings of others

If not helped, children with too many overpowering adults in their lives can think: 'I know what *you* feel, but I have no idea what *I* feel.' Fearful children can be helped to see how they have developed a habit of reacting to the feelings of another while often not even acknowledging their own. As Dan, aged eight, said, 'It's hard for me to be angry, when Daddy is being angry all the time.'

The more children like this can be helped to know what they feel, and then to express these feelings, the stronger and less frightened they will be. Furthermore, finding words for fear, and helping children to think about fear as well as to feel it, can establish lifelong stress-managing systems in their brain.

Helping fearful children to feel empowered in their lives

> Bettelheim noted that the people who survived the extremes of torture and misery in concentration camps were those who managed to find at least one area in which they could experience the self as controller rather than as controlled. (Mollon, 1993, p20)

Talk with the child to find one area in his life, however small, in which he feels in control, potent and not frightened. For example, the child may feel really potent in Maths lessons, as he knows he is good, and can do the sums right. Spend time talking about this, and give it weight in terms of your attention. Another idea is to read him stories in which a fearful child or animal finds their power. Fairy stories are full of children, little animals, tiny elves, dwarves, and trolls who are frightened by people, animals and monsters, but who outwit them with the help of others. For example, Hansel and Gretel are cruelly deceived and abandoned by adults, but through their own cunning and courage, finally win through. Stories of humble heroes defeating something or someone too big and powerful are useful sources of comparison for children who feel locked in fear.

Helping children with rituals or obsessions

If I walk on these cracks in the pavement, then the monsters will get me tonight. (Jamie, aged four.)

The adult must realise that the 'obsessive-compulsive' child feels driven to perform his ritual, as if possessed. It is not a matter of helping him with will-power to stop it. Similarly, if something or someone interrupts the child doing his ritual, say touching railings, and prevents him from completing it, he can feel very desperate, very panicky and very angry. In compulsive ritual, the dangerous feeling has gone into action. To stop the action, the child needs to be helped to move back to feeling safe again. He needs help to speak about his catastrophic fears. He needs someone to understand how awful it is to have these fears, and to understand what is terrifying him so much.

In other words, helping a child to stop his ritual (self-help) means he must be given help to manage his feelings in a better way – help to move from self-regulation to interactive regulation. This means really high-quality empathy and understanding, over time. (Do not expect an overnight cure. Obsessional rituals denote a very strong defence system.) This is where sessions with a child therapist can really help. If a parent wants to help the child herself, it is a question of persuading the child that talking about feelings is a good idea. This is not easy for the obsessive child, who has often moved into obsessions (self-help) from a place of mistrust in the comfort and help of others.

If a child is unconvinced that sharing his feelings with a parent will soothe his distress, and so sticks firmly to his ritual to manage his feelings, the parent may need to look at why the child feels so unsafe about sharing his feelings with her. Sometimes it is because the parent is emotionally blocked in some way – blocking her own fear, perhaps. Then the best thing is for the parent to seek emotional help for herself. A child can feel deeply relieved by this. It is often then that he feels his parent has some emotional space in her mind to help him. Table 2 shows an often very effective behavioural approach to helping children with phobias.

Helping children who suffer from phobias

TABLE 2: BEHAVIOURAL APPROACH TO HELPING CHILDREN WITH PHOBIAS

Diagram A shows the belief about *'What will happen if I don't avoid this awful thing …'* – for example, a spider.

'My belief, if I don't avoid the spider.'

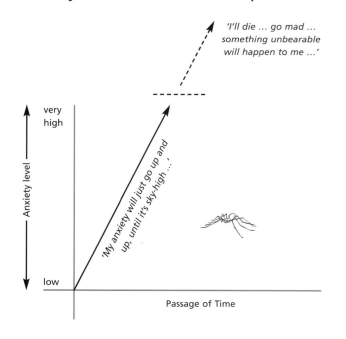

'I'll die … go mad … something unbearable will happen to me …'

My anxiety will just go up and up, until it's sky-high …'

very high

Anxiety level

low

Passage of Time

Diagram B shows what happens when the spider has been avoided. The child feels relieved, and that his avoidance has validated his irrational belief: *'If I hadn't avoided the spider, something terrible would definitely have happened.'* Avoidance therefore actually fuels his fear, and keeps the phobia alive, because it totally supports his irrational belief about the spider being a terrible threat.

Avoidance 'Phew! If I hadn't avoided the spider, something terrible would have happened to me!'

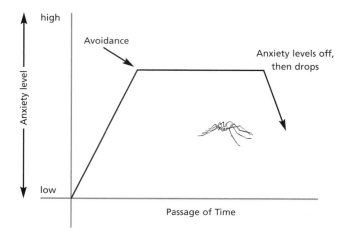

high

Avoidance

Anxiety levels off, then drops

Anxiety level

low

Passage of Time

TABLE 2: *CONTINUED*

Diagram C shows what actually happens if the child dares to stay with the spider, rather than avoiding it.

After a while, his anxiety will actually level off, and then start to go down. The average time this takes is about 20–25 minutes – though the range can be anything between 5 minutes and 1.5 hours – but he will need to stay with the thoughts and feelings that he has about being the room with the spider. If he has the courage to do this repeatedly *and regularly*, then each time his anxiety will go down – and each time it will lessen in intensity until it has eventually disappeared completely, and he no longer has a phobia about spiders. 'Regularly' would mean daily, as opposed to weekly. If, for example, he has a social phobia, then going to a shop once a week would not be enough; ideally, he would need to do it several times a day. But if he dares, the rewards are amazing, and can be quite quick.

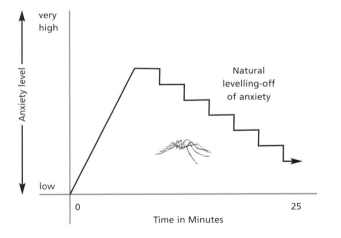

Diagram D shows what happens if a child regularly and consistently faces his fears, day by day.

His anxiety will start to get less and less, and the time it takes for his anxiety to drop will be shorter, until after a while he will no longer have a phobia at all.

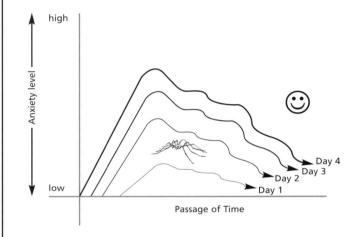

Children need a very benign warm adult to help them through this process, usually a trained psychologist. Forcing them through this process, as opposed to supporting them through it, can make the phobia worsen. Moreover, this is very much a behavioural approach. A therapy which enables the child to understand the true meaning of the phobic object can be equally as effective.

ENABLING CHILDREN TO SPEAK ABOUT AND WORK THROUGH THEIR FEAR

Exercises and tasks for children with fear

This section is designed to provide a whole host of ideas for enabling children to speak about their fear in unthreatening, child-friendly ways. The tasks and exercises are specifically designed to help a child to think about, work through and find a far wider range of healthy options in the face of their fears.

Children often cannot speak clearly and fully about what they are feeling in everyday language, but they can often show or enact, draw or play out their feelings very well indeed. However, they need to be given the right language of expression. For some, this is writing; for others, it is drawing; and for yet others, it might be puppet play, or using miniature toys in a sandbox. Therefore, many of the exercises in this section offer support for creative, imaginative and playful ways of expression. There are also some tasks to ensure that you do not get into asking the fearful child lots of questions, which he may find threatening in itself. So some of the tasks just require a tick in a box; a quick colouring-in; or choosing a word or image from a selection.

Please note: The tasks and exercises are not designed to be worked through in chronological order. Also, there are far too many to attempt them all in one go: the child could feel bombarded. So just pick those you think would be right for the particular child you are working with, taking into account his age, and how defended or undefended he is about talking about his fears.

Instructions to the child, that is, what you might say to him for each exercise, can be found in the tinted boxes.

✰ Prickly person in a ditch

This exercise can be immensely reassuring and empowering to the child who in the past has simply absorbed any rage, hate or over-the-top anger from an adult. The exercise teaches the child to think of ways of protecting himself, which means he can be more detached in the face of an adult who is leaking or discharging all their own unprocessed feelings. It will also enable him to be less vulnerable to the lethal power of shame. The exercise also serves to increase the child's sense of personal boundaries, so providing necessary distance from the fiery feelings of the other.

Next time someone is being cross with you in a frightening way, imagine that in front of you is a huge ditch into which all their critical words fall, so they never really reach you. To practice this, think of a time in the past when you felt awful because someone was criticising you. Look at the first picture.

Figure 20a Prickly person in a ditch

Helping Children with Fear © M Sunderland & N Armstrong 2003

Speechmark

Now move to the next picture. Draw their angry outburst falling down into the ditch and not reaching you.

Figure 20b Prickly person in a ditch

Then look at the third picture. In the speech bubble, write what you would have liked to say or do to that adult who tried to frighten you. Here are some suggestions:

- Put him in a rubbish bin.
- Scribble out his face.
- Paint his nose red.
- Put a zip with a lock on his mouth, so he cannot say cruel or frightening words any more.
- Pour jelly over his head.

Figure 20c Prickly person in a ditch

☆ The gallery of monsters

This exercise enables the fearful child to realise that he does not have to be passive in his response to aggression. It allows the experience of responding, rather than being a victim. It may enable the child to find his anger at being shamed or put down. For fearful children, the following statement is so apt:

> Anger helps us reassert our sense of power and maintain our dignity and self-respect. (Bar-Levav, 1988, p171)

Fearful children desperately need empowering. This exercise therefore, which uses play, humour and absurdity (eg, snakes on the toes), is a great way to start. Anything more direct, less absurd, may just make the fearful child more fearful.

Look at this gallery of monsters. Think of people who you feel have been monsterish to you in your life. Being monsterish means that they have frightened you and made you feel horrible. You can write their names underneath if you like.

Now do what you would like to do to these monsters. You may want to put snakes on their feet, or write 'Stop being a monster to me' on their knees, or put a custard pie on their face. Or maybe you just want to scribble them out entirely.

Figure 21 Gallery of monsters

Speechmark

87

☆ Mad monsters

The aim of this exercise is to enable the child to find his protest under his fear. (So many children who are frightened just move into helpless compliance.)

People are often frightened that if they enable a child in counselling, or in an exercise like this, to find his voice, he will go back home and foolishly take on a violent father. I have never known this. Children who have violent parents are usually very skilled at navigating them.

Are there some people you know, or have known in your life who are so frightening to you they are like mad monsters?

Draw them as mad monsters.

Then mold them in clay or Play-Doh.®

Now do to them what you feel like doing. Once outside your head, instead of inside your head, they can feel far more manageable and far less threatening. You can then take time to think about how you can get help to manage them. You might need some 'togetherness' to deal with them.

Now make an imaginary monster out of clay or Play-Doh®. Make it as scary as you can. You can add teeth and hair and things like that, if you like. Does this monster remind you of anyone in your life who has been monsterish to you? If it does, you might like to write underneath who it reminds you of. Do what you like to your imaginary monster. You might like to keep it just as it is, or squash it, or pull its head off, or squidge it. It is up to you.

✰ Frightened you and not-frightened you

Create two images of yourself in Play-Doh®. The first is *what you feel like* when someone frightens you. The second is *what you would like to feel like* when someone frightens you.

Play on the drum what you would like to feel like if someone is being horrible to you.

✰ Nightmare monsters

Think of a nightmare you have had in which someone or something frightened you.

Draw the nightmare monster.

Now, in your drawing, instead of running away, or being stuck to the spot or whatever, turn and face the monster that is scaring you, and say, *'Here I am – what do you want from me?'*

Write or say what you think the monster's response would be. Then do what you want to the frightening monster. You can throw your monster in the bin if you like. Or you could try saying, 'I will not let you hurt me', or 'NO, NO, NO', or 'How dare you try to frighten me!', or something you would like to say or shout at him.

☆ Nightmare happenings

Have you ever had any of these things happen to you in a nightmare? If so, tick the picture or colour it in.

Figure 22a
Nightmare
happenings

If it is something else, draw your own nightmare happening in the empty box.

Figure 22b
Nightmare
happenings

☆ Nightmare with a different ending

Draw a nightmare you have had, but this time give the nightmare a different ending. It is fine to have someone help you in your nightmare, so that it turns from a nightmare into a dream with a good ending.

✮ Worry head

Look at the worry head. All the worries are numbered from one to ten. Ten is the largest worry in your life, and one is the smallest. So ten is a very big worry in your life that will not go away, and one is a little worry. Five is a medium-sized worry.

Draw or write your worries on the worry head. It is always important to get help from kind grown-ups with number five to number ten. Also you might find that something you think is just a little worry is actually more than that, and you are just telling yourself it is a little worry when in fact it is a big one!! Do you have any worries like that? A grown-up can help you if you do.

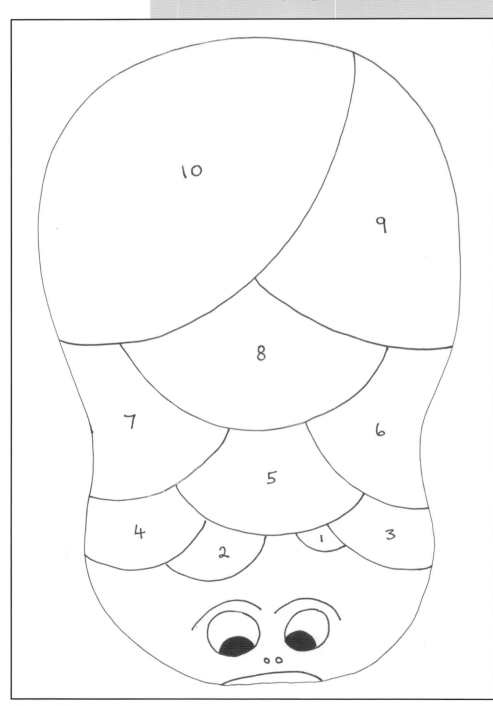

Figure 23
Worry head

✮ When fear gets you

The only thing we have to fear is fear itself. (Roosevelt, 1933, Presidential Inaugural Address)

When you are frightened, do you feel like any of these people in the pictures?

If you do, colour in or tick the particular picture. It can be more than one picture.

Like a tiny lonely speck	In a bottomless pit	Being shot at	Being crushed
Drowning in a swirling river	In a world full of monsters	A person without a mouth	

Figure 24 When fear gets you

If you do not feel like any of these, draw in the empty box what you do feel like when fear gets you.

✰ Feel the fear and do it anyway

This exercise is designed for the child who has a challenge coming up in life, the thought of which he is finding very scary – for example, dancing in a show or running a big race. The exercise can be a *very* powerful mental rehearsal for moving forwards towards the challenge and dealing with it, rather than walking away from it, or giving up on it. It is a vital life-skill too.

Think of something in your life you really want to do, but which you are afraid of doing. Grown-ups call this a 'challenge'.

Then imagine your fears about this challenge as the fear hoop in the picture. Draw yourself on the steps, facing your fear hoop. You can add things to your fear hoop if you like.

Now draw yourself walking through the fear hoop to the 'DONE IT' sign. Draw yourself being successful in your challenge.

What did you feel, moving through the fear up to the 'DONE IT' sign?

What did you feel drawing yourself being successful?

Figure 25 Feel the fear and do it anyway

✩ Scary yucky things

Here are some things that lots of people find scary. Do you find any of them scary? Colour in the ones that you do. If there is something else that really scares you, and it is not on the list, draw it in the empty box.

Bugs	Injections (at the dentist's or doctor's)	Police	Loud noises
Snakes	Spiders	Worms	An apple with maggots in it
Someone calling you horrid names	Bullies	Being on your own	Ghosts
Burglars	Monsters	Dreams of being chased	Scary grown-ups
Scary films	Sharks	Scary stories	

Figure 26

Scary yucky things

Speechmark ⑤ Ⓟ *Helping Children with Fear* © M Sunderland & N Armstrong 2003   **95**

✩ Stuck to the spot with fear

When you are frightened, if you could do what any of these animals can do, which would you choose? Colour in the one you have chosen.

An ostrich with its head in the sand	A tortoise pulling back into its shell	A hedgehog rolling up into a ball
A stick insect camouflaging into the twig	A rabbit rushing down a deep hole	Help box

Figure 27 Stuck to the Spot with Fear

Then draw, in the help box, the person or thing you would need to help you move out of this hiding place and deal with the thing you are frightened of.

✩ Safe forts

I would live happy
in an ivy bush
high in some twisted tree
and never come out…

(Heaney, from 'Sweeney Astray',
1990, pp135–6)

When people or things are frightening, which of these following hiding places would you like?

Colour in the ones you would like, or draw yourself there. If it is none of these, draw in the last box what other safe place you would like to be in.

A tunnel	A den	Your bed	A walled fortress where nobody can get you
A mummy's tummy – just like a baby again	A hole in the ground	A secret place you do not want me to know about	A tree house
An island – so no-one could get to you	On the moon	Behind the sofa	

Then think about who or what you would like to come into your hiding place.

Figure 28 Safe forts

☆ Super getaways

When you are frightened, which of these would you most like to have, or to do?

A super-fast car	A hot air balloon	An ejector button
An invisible cloak	A helicopter	Going into a completely new world
A speedboat	A genie in a lamp	

Figure 29 Super getaways

If it is none of these, draw in the empty box what you would like to have as your super getaway.

☆ 'Stop' power

Without help, many frightened children cannot get in touch with their anger at the person who frightened them. They are so locked in fear that they are often totally out of touch with the fact that they might be angry at how frightened they have been made to feel. Anger makes a child feel stronger. Without being able to be angry or assertive, children will inevitably feel frightened.

Role-play being beastly to the child. You can do it in a funny way to start with, so that you do not actually frighten him. Get him to say 'STOP' to you. Carry on until he has real confidence and power in his voice, then stop. The child practises saying 'STOP' to you, with his hand and his words. You may need to model this to the child at first, until he feels emotionally empowered enough to do it on his own.

This is very good for making children realise they have rights, and for establishing a clear response if someone is being unkind, or frightening in some way.

Play the 'STOP' game with drums.

This will enable the child to connect with a real sense of protest: 'I will not be treated like this, I deserve better.'

☆ The yes/no game

This is a great game for children who are too scared of someone else's anger and protest to be able to find their own. The slow change in volume allows them to go to the pitch they can stand.

> Every time I say 'Yes', you say 'No'. We will start quietly, but each time make your 'No' a little bit louder than my 'Yes', until eventually we both sound very loud!

✩ From Lonely Island to Together City

Look at the picture, while thinking about the worrying or scary things in your life at the moment. Do you feel like you are on Lonely Island, in the Small Help Zone or in Together City?

Draw the place on the picture where you usually go to when things are worrying or frightening. Draw yourself as a dot. For example, if you do the worrying all on your own without telling anyone, draw a dot on Lonely Island. If you ask for a bit of help, draw yourself on Small Help Zone. If you are really good at getting help, draw yourself in Together City.

If you have drawn yourself on Lonely Island, draw yourself getting to Together City. How do you get there? Who or what helps you? What do you do there? All the people in Together City are kind grown-ups who can help you.

It is a really clever thing to be able to ask for help when something is too worrying, too hard or too frightening.

Figure 30 From Lonely Island to Together City

☆ Struggle story

Finish the story:

There was a boy/girl with a struggle inside them ....

....

The struggle was called ....

....

The boy/girl had been struggling with the struggle for a long time.
For .... (How long?)

Then one day the boy/girl decided they were so miserable that
they needed help ....

....

So they went to see .... (It can be a real
person or a fantasy person, or a person in a film, eg, Harry Potter.)

And .... (the chosen person) said ....

....

So together they dealt with the struggle by ....

....

....

....

....

....

....

....

✰ Fighting volcanoes

This exercise is relevant for children who have witnessed traumatic parental arguments or parental violence.

Once, Rex was watching some volcanoes, that he liked very much, having a very big row with each other. And when they rowed, it made a storm and a wind and too much rain, and a flood and a fire all at the same time. The thing was, no-one was thinking about how scary it was for Rex.

What it made Rex feel was (tick which you think):

⊚ Too sad ☐

⊚ Too lonely ☐

⊚ Too angry ☐

⊚ Too helpless ☐

⊚ Screaming inside ☐

⊚ Badly wanting it to stop but he couldn't make it stop. ☐

Write in the speech bubble in the picture what Rex wanted to say to the volcanoes.

Figure 31

Fighting volcanoes

☆ When grown-ups argue

This exercise is a different version of the above. It enables children to have a voice about a situation in which they may have had no voice.

> When grown-ups in your life argue, or when you see a grown-up being unkind to a child, it can feel like you are watching a terrible storm, or war, or nightmare.
>
> Draw or write here what you would want to say to the arguing or unkind grown-up.
>
> If it helps, you can imagine yourself as someone like Batman, Superman or Harry Potter.
>
> You may want to draw who you would want to be there helping you with the arguing grown-ups, as often there is just you, and it can feel far too lonely and far too sad and far too alone.

☆ Friendly monster

> Draw a friendly monster.
>
> Befriend your monster and get him to help you with something you are finding frightening. The next poem might help you draw your friendly monster.

I fell in love with an alien being
Whose skin was jelly, whose teeth were green
She had big bug eyes and the death ray glare
Feet like water wings, purple hair.

(Cooper Clarke, 1979, p43)

✩ What do you fear most?

Tick the ones that apply:

- ◉ Being hated by a grown-up? ☐
- ◉ Not being good enough? ☐
- ◉ Being told off for doing something bad? ☐
- ◉ Being told off for doing something wrong? ☐
- ◉ Something happening to your Mum or Dad? ☐
- ◉ Being bullied? ☐
- ◉ Needing help and no-one coming? ☐
- ◉ Losing the people you love the most? ☐

If none of these apply, write or draw what you fear most.

✩ Good power

A man found himself slipping too often into the role of Little Me. So we worked on Little Me, and found that this character was very much one of those caught in the double bind of parental approval/disapproval. He was encouraged to break through this by repeated role-playing... The difference was positive and very striking. And when asked which of his sub-personalities was now coming into play, the man replied, 'Tiger'. (Rowan, 1990, p52)

Try drawing yourself as something powerful, such as a tiger, a sun or a wolf. As this creature or being, what would you do all day? Who would you like to feel power over, or powerful with? What would you be feeling, what would you do, what would you enjoy? Draw all this. What steps can you put in place to make some of this in some way come true in your life?

✰ Life change

Draw a 'Keep Forever' box and a 'Throw Out Now' box. Draw, in your Keep Forever box, all the things about your life that you like and all the people that you like. In your 'Throw Out Now' box, put all the things and people you wish were not in your life. You can throw away feelings, people, problems etc. How can you get help with the things in your 'Throw Out Now' box so you do not keep trying to manage them all on your own.

✩ Frightening grown-ups

Is there a grown-up you know who, when they get angry, is like one of the things below? If so, colour it in.

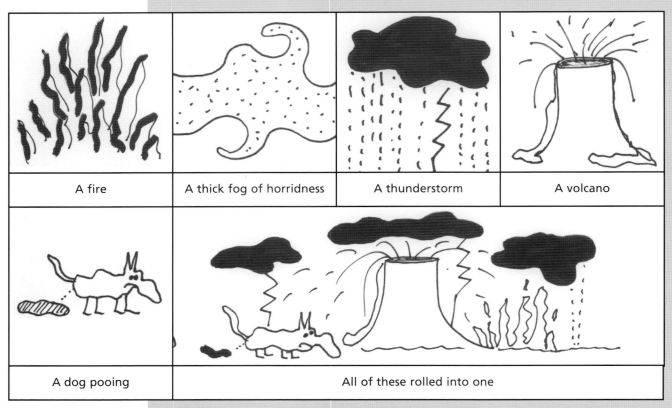

A fire	A thick fog of horridness	A thunderstorm	A volcano
A dog pooing	All of these rolled into one		

Figure 32
Frightening grown-ups

Who or what would you like to help you with this angry grown-up, so you didn't feel so alone? Draw them helping you. In your picture, what happens to the angry grown-up when you get help?

If you had magic words, or magic powers to help you with it, what would they be?

☆ The horrid house or help garden

When life is too frightening, you have a big choice to make. Do you stay in a horrid place like the horrid house in this picture with no help, or do you go into a place like the help garden in the picture? No-one needs to be alone. There are always kind adults in the world who can help.

If you have ever asked for help when something has been too difficult or frightening, colour in one of the flowers in the help garden. If you have asked for help more than once, colour in more than one flower. It is so smart that you asked for help. If you have never asked for help, draw yourself in the horrid house. What stops you using the help garden? Who could help you to move into the garden?

Figure 33 The horrid house or the help garden

✩ When you fear your own fear

Draw yourself doing one or more of these things:

◎ Fighting a monster

◎ Battling with a terrible, swirling, powerful river

◎ Standing up to a frightening grown-up

◎ Standing up to an imaginary roaring snippercracker.

Now draw someone with you in each of the pictures. It may be a friend, or it may be a big safe grown-up who helps you by saying things like, 'Stop, you are a bully!', or 'It is always wrong to hurt or frighten children; children have a right to feel safe.'

✫ Feeling muddles and messes

When something is too frightening in your life, or too difficult to think about properly, it can feel as if you have a mess or muddle of feelings inside you.

If you know this feeling, draw the mess or muddle of feelings inside you. If it is in your tummy, draw it in your tummy. If it feels like it's in your head, draw it in your head. If it feels like it is in both, draw it in both. If you like, you can add bits of Play-Doh®, or clay or gluey bits of things – wood or string – to your mess, to show exactly what your mess feels like

Then draw what you would like to do to the feeling mess, or the help you need to help you with the feeling mess. .

☆ Genie help

Think of something very scary that has happened to you.

Figure 34
Genie help

If you had had a genie at the time, what would your three wishes have been? Write them in the three wish bubbles.

☆ Tom Thumb was great

Right in the middle of the flower, on the green centre, sat a little tiny girl, graceful and delicate as a fairy. She was no more than a thumb-joint high, and so she was called Thumbelina. (Andersen, 1994, pp14–15)

Some fairy-tale people are very clever. Even though they are small, they have still managed to think of really big things to do. The tiny Thumbelina has to trust and rely on the kindness of animals to house and feed her. The Babes in the Wood are cruelly deceived and abandoned by adults, but finally win through. The seven dwarves are the kindly creatures who rescue Snow White from the threatening, wicked stepmother.

Imagine you are small like Tom Thumb or Thumbelina, but very, very, very clever. What would you do with the frightened things in these pictures? Draw on the pictures what you could do to stop them from being frightening?

| A monster under the bed | A bully |
| Watching another child being bullied | A frightening grown-up |

Figure 35 Tom Thumb was great

Now finish the story:

One upon a time there was a very, very small .... (draw him)

He felt very sad and frightened that he was so small.

So one day he ....

And then what happened was ....

And ....

And ....

Until in the end he ....

Then do a story based on Teenie Weenie.

Once Teenie Weenie wandered into a very frightening forest.

And what happened to him there was ....

So what he did was ....

And in the end he ....

☆ What makes you feel really safe in the world?

Tick if any of these make you feel really safe in the world.

- ◎ When I am on my own. ☐
- ◎ When I am with .... (write the person's name) ☐
- ◎ When I am in my bedroom. ☐
- ◎ When I am in my bed. ☐
- ◎ When I am with my friends. ☐
- ◎ When I am with one of my parents. ☐
- ◎ When I am in school. ☐
- ◎ When I am not in school. ☐

If it is none of these, draw what makes you feel safe.

☆ Fear sticks

Draw on each of the fear sticks a time when you were really frightened, and no-one was there to help you with your fear. We have drawn in some examples to help you.

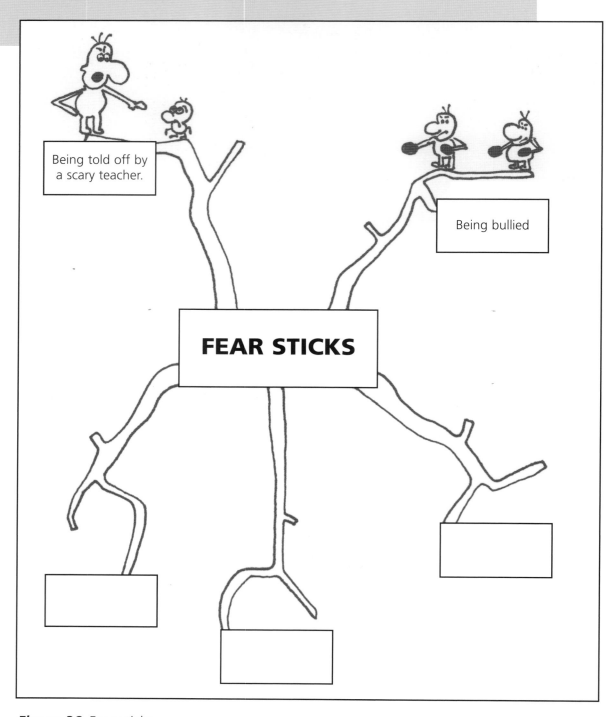

Figure 36 Fear sticks

✫ Your heroes

For fearful children, having the time and space to talk about their heroes and heroines can often re-kindle their lost or fragile sense of there being enough goodness in the world. Be aware of how these role models may nurture a child, or encourage a child to overcome feelings of impotence or fear.

> Draw, or write, or tell about a person you really admire. It can be a real person, or a person in a story, or in a film, or on TV. If they could be your friend, how might they help you with things in your life that frighten you? What might they say or do?

CONSIDERING COUNSELLING OR THERAPY FOR FEARFUL CHILDREN

What can be the long-term effects for the children who do not get help in addressing their fears?

Without help, the frightened, anxious child may all too easily develop into a frightened, anxious adult. Life is still experienced as a threat, blighted by all manner of catastrophising thoughts and fantasies, fears of being shamed, criticised, or frightened all over again. Put simply, without help fearful children can become people-phobic for life. Their fears can be generalised (GAD – generalised anxiety disorder). In this case, the fear of certain people in childhood – for example, teachers and parents – is generalised to many situations and people in later life.

> **Sarah**
> In Sarah's childhood, her father had exploded with rage on a regular basis. When she grew up, she said she could never relax, or look forward to anything, because this might be the day when someone criticised her, or shouted at her. In therapy, she remembered instances of shaking with terror at the frightening and hating face of her father.

As we have seen, if a child is repeatedly subjected to frightening experiences, he can develop a trigger-happy amygdala (alarm system) in the lower brain. This means overreactions of fear and anxiety in response to even the most minor stressors, which other people would just take in their stride. This can continue throughout life, unless there is therapeutic intervention to help the child work through his fear. In other words, without counselling or therapy, fear, anxiety and agitation can all too easily establish themselves as actual personality traits. This means the child grows into a perpetually anxious adult, never knowing inner calm.

Due to the plasticity of the higher brain, it is not too late to establish stress-regulatory systems and chemical balances that will enable a fearful child to know true calm for the first time in his life. But to shift hard-wiring and chemical balances set on fear and worry takes a very powerful input – an input equivalent to the consistently calming, soothing attention of a mother with her baby. For some children whose brain has been hard-wired for a fearful response, it takes this kind of relational experience in therapy to effect change. This often means therapy more than once a week.

How therapy can help fearful children to know a warmer world

The following is a delightful explanation of why therapy is needed for the traumatised child:

> A terrible trauma has occurred in early childhood, inflicted on the passive and innocent child from the outside (a disgruntled fairy). The terror and helplessness of this traumatic event remain embedded in the heart of the personality, awaiting a call back to life by a more hospitable environment. The self of the [child] is ultimately passive; lack of good [nurturing] produces a retreat to a lifeless withdrawal, until the [therapist] (the prince) awakens it from its slumber. (Guntrip, 1969, p10)

Therapy can indeed be a 'call back' to life. It can enable the child – perhaps for the first time – to experience a truly warm world, as opposed to a threatening one.

Every child needs someone to talk to about their fears and anxieties

> Before I went to counselling, I had always thought that fear was something you just had to deal with by yourself. (Edward, aged 13)

As we have seen, the problem is that for lots of children who are fearful, the last thing they think of doing is telling someone they are scared. Some children only 'wake up' to the fact that they are basically people-phobic through therapy. For many children, it only becomes possible to really acknowledge to themselves that they are frightened, and so to face up to their fears for the very first time, *in the presence of an empathic other*. One boy said, prior to seeing a counsellor, 'I am scared of nothing', then as the therapy progressed, he told his counsellor, 'I am scared of everything.'

Figure 37 depicts the mind of a fearful child before and after a successful therapy. Before therapy, a child can be plagued with monsters in his mind – monsters in the form of perceived or actual threats. After therapy, when each of these threats, real or imagined, have been thought about and felt, the child's inner world no longer needs to be haunted by such fears. In fact, his inner world becomes a warmer place as the empathic, compassionate therapist is internalised as a symbol of kindness and concern.

Figure 37 Before and after therapy

For some children who have real threats in their life – like a father who hits them, or a mother who is psychologically cruel – the therapist can become the lifeline the child never had. A good therapist will be perceived as someone 'safe'; as a comforter, advocate and ally. The child's inner world becomes a far safer place because of this relationship, and so his external world can feel far more manageable.

How counselling or therapy can help a frightened child find his voice, often for the very first time

Space is where tininess goes. (Hill, 1993, p36)

Sophie, aged eight

Sophie had a dream of a big mountain with a tiny little girl on top. Through talking to her counsellor, she realised that the huge mountain was actually a mountain of her own unexpressed anger towards the grown-ups in her life who had frightened her. She had been denying these angry feelings to herself, so the mountain felt terrifying. After acknowledging the fear of her own rage, this split between the tiny, frightened part of herself and the 'huge, frightening mountain rage force' was lessened. Sophie was then able, with support from her therapist, to confront some of the frightening adults.

Figure 38 Big mountain with little, tiny girl on top

Counselling or therapy can help a frightened child build up a stronger self

Psychotherapy can 'help someone to defend or attack without disproportionate emotional tension.' (Horney, 1977, p251)

Psychotherapy can help fearful children to build up a more resilient self and healthier defences and to know 'that even if our situation is less than perfect, most of the time we are not in real danger' (Bar-Levav, 1988, p127).

Counselling or therapy can help a child to build up healthier, more creative ways of protecting himself. Phobias and obsessions, for example, are unhealthy ways of self-protecting: as we have seen, they have too high a price. But being enabled to confront someone (perhaps with necessary help) who is the source of your fear is healthy. For some children, facing a fear in therapy can be the first step in beating the impulse to flee.

Emmanuel, aged ten

Emmanuel had been hit by his mother for several years. He suffered from all manner of phobias and obsessions. He went to see the school counsellor, and in counselling he realised that it was not normal for children to get beaten. He asked the therapist to see him with his mother. With the therapist present, he felt confident enough to say to his mother, 'I want you to throw away the stick. You scare me too much, and it makes me hate you.' The mother was so moved by his eloquence that she threw away the stick. Emmanuel's phobias and obsessions stopped.

Michael, aged fifteen

Michael had been paranoid for years. He experienced the world as a deeply threatening place. He did not dare walk past the town hall in the morning, because he thought that the stone statues of lions there were always looking at him with terrible hate and rage. In therapy, he owned up to his own intense, lion-like rage towards his father, who had beaten him regularly. After that the stone lions meant nothing to him: they were just stone lions.

Toby, aged eight

Toby suffered from terrible nightmares. His mother had been very depressed, and Toby was over-compliant with her. He was very frightened that his feelings might hurt her, because she was so fragile. One day in therapy, Toby talked of his recurring nightmare of a bull kicking him relentlessly. However, while he was telling the nightmare he started to flick sand at the therapist. The therapist asked, 'I wonder if you are wanting to get through to me with the sand?' When the boy realised that the kicking dream was his own wish to kick his mother, to get a response out of her, he cried about his loneliness. On owning up to his grief and his helpless rage, his nightmares stopped.

Counselling or therapy can equip a child with a vocabulary of assertion

Sometimes children need to find a vocabulary of assertion in order to empower themselves. Without the words, they cannot begin to think about how they might confront someone in their life who is being cruel or mean. A child can feel much stronger in the safety of the therapeutic environment, when he can rehearse assertive responses to those by whom he feels threatened.

Counselling and therapy can bring a real sense of relief from speaking about a fear that has been locked up inside for years

When you tell your deepest, darkest secrets and people don't recoil in horror, like you think they would, you become healed. (Jeffers, 1992, p117)

Some fearful children find therapy an immense relief, in terms of expressing feelings and fears that have been locked up inside their body and mind for far too long, causing all manner of debilitating emotional handicaps in their life. One little girl, who had been locked in a cupboard in a boarding school when she was naughty, came to therapy, and let out the screams of fear about her experience week after week after week. It was clear that, in the cupboard, she had cut off from her fear, moving into a state of numbing dissociation.

Working with children who find the therapy itself a frightening experience

> To be understood correctly is to be engulfed, to be enclosed, swallowed up, drowned, eaten up, smothered, stifled in or by another person's supposed all-embracing comprehension. (Laing, 1990, p 45)

For some fearful children, counselling or therapy can initally be very difficult. They have too much mistrust of adults. The therapy can re-trigger a sense of someone 'seeing through', or 'seeing into' them or getting too close. Or the child can assume a repeat of the judging, shaming or demanding attention he has experienced previously. All this may make him want to close off from, rather than open up to, the therapist.

> Where there is a fear that no-one can help in an utterly damaged and persecuting world, where any attempts to 'get through' are experienced as a violent attack, help itself may be warded off violently. (Segal, 1985, p171)

Jamie, aged ten

Jamie had suffered from several traumas of invasion in his life. In therapy, he said to me that he was worried that I would 'turn him into something else, and would forget to turn him back again'. He found a little witch in the box of toys to represent me.

With such children it is necessary to work slowly and gently; to empathise with their defences, talking about trust and mistrust. You might show – through a picture or sandplay image – that you can appreciate why the child might indeed not trust you in the light of how some grown-ups have treated him in the past. If this can be talked about and worked through, it can alter the child's entire belief system about people and life as being essentially dangerous.

We see below how Casement, a psychoanalyst, expresses his empathy with a client who is frightened by the experience of therapy itself:

'When I imagine being in your place, with all those questions coming at me, I feel as if someone were trying to get inside me – forcing me to give away bits of myself that I might not want to give away.' (Silence.) 'I have an image of being surrounded by people trying to force me to talk, and wanting to hide from them. I can also imagine myself not talking to anyone, as a way of trying to build a wall around me to keep people out... you might be needing to keep up a wall of silence as a way of keeping me out and at a safe distance.' (Casement, 1985, pp54–5)

The child must be given time to find out that the therapist is safe and worthy of his trust. Again, to quote Casement, the therapist needs to be:

A presence that is neither intrusively present nor traumatically absent... Thus the patient can begin to reach out, to find and to use the [therapist] in whatever way... (Casement, 1990, p95)

Counselling or therapy can offer the child a safe environment in which to grieve about all the times he was frightened and no-one knew or helped

Children who have known a life of too much fear need to mourn the times they have spent feeling too alone with their fear; the times when they so desperately needed help, and didn't get it; and the times they did not even think of asking for help, because they had already established a way of being in the world, which is to do frightening things on their own. In short, therapy can bring to an end the solitary struggle a child has had with his fear.

But is therapy or counselling a waste of time if the child has to go back to a frightening household?

[The therapist] pays close attention to every word I say, as if what I am saying is of the utmost importance. (Thrail, 1994, p46)

This is a very common question, but the answer is a clear 'No' because therapy brings the fearful child so many profoundly good experiences. Therapy can mean:

⭐ A fearful child finding his voice, often for the first time.

⭐ The consistent experience of kindness and concern, sometimes for the first time.

⭐ The experience of having someone emotionally strong enough and present enough to be with all your feelings.

⭐ The experience of being heard, seen and valued – sometimes for the first time.

Therapy is not about changing the child's outer world (this is for the social workers, where appropriate). It is about changing the child's inner world – in the case of the frightened child, changing their inner world from a hostile, threatening one, to one with hope and warmth, and a knowledge of real compassion and concern. It is the inner world that colours perception, just as much as, and sometimes more than, the outer world – the external realities of the child's life.

Table 3 on page 125 shows what can happen if the fearful child is not helped.

TABLE 3: IF THE FEARFUL CHILD IS LEFT UNHELPED: THE COMMON LEGACIES FOR ADULTHOOD

Fears which are generalized to many situations	Wants and needs
☆ Loss of boundaries ☆ Contamination ☆ Loss of identity ☆ Loss of power ☆ Engulfment: loss of self and identity ☆ No escape routes, or means of escape ☆ Nowhere to hide	☆ A lot of space away from people, and major periods of time on your own. ☆ To know that other people are really safe. ☆ Respect for your safety in distance. ☆ To be allowed to go away or withdraw and know that friends and partners will still love you and wait for you to come back. ☆ If there have to be heavy social periods, there will often be a real pull to balance them with substantial time on one's own.
Beliefs and fallacies	**Use of space and negotiation of social interactions**
☆ 'Life and people are often unsafe and/or frightening. They will overwhelm you and defeat you.' ☆ 'If you let someone get close, you cannot escape; they will get inside you, overwhelm you, control you or take you away.' ☆ 'If a relationship gets too close, then you have to do something to get the safe space you need, like start a big row.' ☆ 'Committed relationships are about being trapped and losing your freedom.' ☆ 'To stay safe, I need to control all my relationships and my entire environment.' ☆ 'Other people, their mess and noise, their very presence, suffocate me.'	☆ Need to move through daily life in a way in which you can avoid people. Many people are seen as obstacles to be avoided. ☆ Need for order to keep people out. ☆ Defence in flight: cutting off feelings to cut off from the world. ☆ A tendency to become secretive and distant. ☆ Impossible to get on the telephone, at times trying in some sense not to be there, 'unavailable'. ☆ Irrationally, sometimes the physical presence of others in public places – eg, in cars on the road, or in a bank or café – can feel like a gross intrusion on their space. ☆ Rejecting by pushing away, or just not being there.

TABLE 3: *CONTINUED*	
Beliefs and fallacies *(continued)*	
✭ 'Closeness carries obligations to please or take care of others.' ✭ 'Space is "friendly expanses dotted more or less densely with dangerous unpredictable objects"' (Balint, 1955, p228).	
Relationships	**Behavioural set-up of reinforcement of beliefs**
✭ Merger experienced as extremely dangerous. ✭ Closeness experienced as a threat of being taken over, or sucked dry. ✭ Always finding reasons for 'must be going' and not staying. ✭ Overreaction. 'If you ask for something, I hear it as a demand.' ✭ Fear of being stolen from or emptied out by the other.	✭ Being withdrawn can often lead to attack from others. Retreating, can often lead to others advancing, and subtly an invitation for others to move in, as more space has been made available. ✭ Staying silent to ward off invasion, actually often gets people to invade you with questions.
Common vocabulary	**Areas of safety**
✭ Stifling, suffocating, noise, mess, tied down, no room, trapped, demanding; 'I need more space.' ✭ Some people who fear invasion often make statements about overpopulation, there being too many immigrants etc.	✭ Open space – without people. ✭ Retreat in one's own home. ✭ Small, confined womb-like spaces without people.
Fairy stories preferred	**Fundamental unrealised reality**
✭ Wizard of Oz ✭ Superman } quick-escape heroes ✭ Peter Pan	✭ If you let people get close, you can always move away again whenever you want.

RECOMMENDED READING

Bloch D, 1978, *'So the Witch Won't Eat Me': Fantasy and the Child's Fear of Infanticide*, Grove Press, New York.

Blume ES, 1990, *Secret Survivors: Uncovering Incest and its After-effects in Women*, John Wiley, Chichester/New York.

Bowlby J, 1988, *A Secure Base – Clinical Applications of Attachment Theory*, Routledge, London.

Holland S & Ward C, 1990, *Assertiveness: A Practical Approach*, Speechmark Publishing, Bicester.

Jeffers S, 1987, *Feel the Fear and Do it Anyway*, Arrow, London.

Miller A, 1987, *For Your Own Good: The Roots of Violence in Child-Rearing*, Hannum H & H (trans), Virago, London.

Sarnoff D with Moore G, 1987, *Never Be Nervous Again*, Century, London.

Steiner J, 1993, *Psychic Retreats: Pathological Organizations in Psychotic, Neurotic and Borderline Patients*, Routledge/Institute of Psychoanalysis, London.

Williams G, 1997, *Internal Landscapes and Foreign Bodies. Eating Disorders and Other Pathologies*, Duckworth, London.

BIBLIOGRAPHY

Andersen HC, 1994, *Hans Andersen's Fairy Tales*, Lewis N (trans), Puffin, Harmondsworth. (Original work published 1846.)

Anderson R (ed), 1992, *Clinical Lectures on Klein and Bion*, Routledge, London.

Balint E, 1993, *Before I Was I: Psychoanalysis and the Imagination*, Mitchell J & Parsons M (eds), Free Association Books, London.

Balint M, 1955, 'Friendly Expanses – Horrid Empty Spaces', *International Journal of Psycho-Analysis*, 36 (4/5): 225–41.

Bar-Levav R, 1988, *Thinking in the Shadow of Feelings*, Simon & Schuster, New York.

Beebe B & Lachmann F, 1988, 'The Contribution of Mother-Infant Mutual Influence to the Origins of Self- and Object Representations', *Psychoanalytic Psychology* 5 (4), pp305–37.

Berne E, 1979, *What Do You Say After You Say Hello?*, Bantam, New York. (Original work published 1972.)

Blume ES, 1990, *Secret Survivors: Uncovering Incest and its After-effects in Women*, John Wiley, Chichester/New York.

Bollas C, 1987, *The Shadow of the Object: Psychoanalysis of the Unknown Thought*, Free Association Books, London.

Bowlby J, 1973, *Attachment and Loss: Volume 2 – Separation, Anxiety and Anger*, Hogarth Press, London.

Bowlby J, 1988, *A Secure Base: Clinical Applications of Attachment Theory*, Routledge, London.

Carroll L, 1994, *Alice'sc Adventures in Wonderland*. Penguin, Harmondsworth.

Casement P, 1985, *On Learning From the Patient*, Routledge, London.

Casement P, 1990, *Further Learning from the Patient: The Analytic Space and Process*, Tavistock/Routledge, London.

Children's Act (1989) Children's Services Planning Order, The Stationery Office Books, London.

Clarkson P, 1989, *Gestalt Counselling in Action*, Sage, London.

Cooper Clarke J, 1979, *Directory 1979*, Omnibus, London.

Dickens C, 1995, *Great Expectations*, Penguin/Puffin, Harmondsworth. (Original work published 1861.)

Dryden W & Gordon J, 1994, *How to Cope When the Going Gets Tough*, Sheldon Press, London.

Dumont, R, 1996, *The Sky is Falling*, WW Norton & Co, New York.

Euripedes, 1994, *Plays: One (Medea: The Phoenician Women)*, Methuen, London.

Freud S, 1979a, 'Repression', *On Metapsychology: The Theory of Psychoanalysis*, *The Penguin Freud Library Vol 11*, Richards A & Strachey J (eds), Strachey J (trans), Penguin, Harmondsworth, pp139–57. (Original work published 1915.)

Freud S, 1979b, 'Inhibitions, Symptoms and Anxiety', *On Psychopathology, Inhibitions, Symptoms and Anxiety*, *The Penguin Freud Library Vol 10*, Richards A & Strachey J (eds), Strachey J (trans), Penguin, Harmondsworth, pp237–333. (Original work published 1926.)

Freud S, 1979c, 'Anxiety and Instinctual Life', *New Introductory Lectures on Psychoanalysis*, *The Penguin Freud Library*, *Vol 2,* Richards A & Strachey J (eds), Strachey J (trans), Penguin, Harmondsworth, pp113–44. (Original work published 1933.)

Gibson W, 1993, *Virtual Light*, Penguin, Harmondsworth.

Glouberman D, 1989, *Life Choices and Life Changes Through Imagework: The Art of Developing Personal Vision*, Unwin Hyman, London.

Goleman D, 1996, *Emotional Intelligence*, Bloomsbury, London.

Greenberg JR & Mitchell SA, 1983, *Object Relations in Psychoanalytic Theory*, Harvard University Press, London/Cambridge, MA.

Guntrip H, 1969, *Schizoid Phenomena, Object-Relations and the Self*, Hogarth, London.

Heaney S, 1990, *New Selected Poems 1966–1987,* Faber & Faber, London.

Herman N, 1987, *Why Psychotherapy?,* Free Association Books, London.

Herman N, 1988, *My Kleinian Home: A Journey Through Four Psychotherapies*, Free Association Books, London.

Hill S, 1993, *A Little Book of Meat*, Bloodaxe, Newcastle.

Hinshelwood RD, 1989, *A Dictionary of Kleinian Thought*, Free Association Books, London.

Horney K, 1977, *The Neurotic Personality of Our Time*, Routledge, London. (Original work published 1937.)

Hughes T, 1970, *The Hawk in the Rain*, Faber & Faber, London. (Original work published 1957.)

Jeffers S, 1987, *Feel the Fear and Do It Anyway*, Arrow, London.

Jeffers S, 1992, *Dare to Connect*, Piatkus, London.

Johnson SM, 1994, *Character Styles*, Norton, New York.

Kafka F, 1981, *Stories 1904–1924*, Underwood JA (trans), Futura, London.

Kafka F, 1992, *Metamorphosis and Other Stories*, Muir E & Muir W (trans), Minerva, London. (Original work published 1933.)

Keenan B, 1992, *An Evil Cradling*, Vintage, London.

Klein M, 1975a, 'On the Theory of Anxiety and Guilt', *The Writings of Melanie Klein: Vol. 3 – Envy and Gratitude and Other Works 1946–1963*, Hogarth Press, London, pp25–42. (Original work published 1950.)

Klein M, 1975b, 'On Mental Health', *The Writings of Melanie Klein: Vol. 3 – Envy and Gratitude and Other Works 1946–1963*, Hogarth Press, London, pp268–74. (Original work published 1960.)

Kohut H, 1977, *The Restoration of the Self*, International Universities Press, New York.

Laing RD, 1967, *The Politics of Experience & the Bird of Paradise*, Penguin, Harmondsworth.

Laing RD, 1970, *Knots*, Pantheon, New York.

Laing RD, 1990, *The Divided Self*, Penguin, Harmondsworth. (Original work published 1959.)

Le Doux J, 1998, *The Emotional Brain*, Weidenfeld & Nicolson, London.

Marks IM, 1971, 'Phobic Disorders Four Years After Treatment: A Prospective Follow-Up', *British Journal of Psychiatry*, 118: 683–8.

May R, 1976, *The Courage to Create*, Bantam, New York.

Miller A, 1987, *For Your Own Good: The Roots of Violence in Child-Rearing*, Hannum H & H (trans), Virago, London.

Mollon P, 1993, *The Fragile Self: The Structure of Narcissistic Disturbance*, Whurr, London.

Morton M, 1995, *The Tunnel*, Yale University Press, New Haven/London.

Murray L, 1988, 'Effects of Postnatal Depression on Infant Development: Direct Studies of Early Mother-Infant Reactions', Kumar R & Brockington IF (eds), *Motherhood and Mental Illness 2: Causes and Consequences*, Wright, London/Boston, pp159–90.

Murray L, 1997, *Subhuman Redneck Poems,* Carcanet, Manchester.

Nakhla F & Jackson G, 1993, *Picking Up the Pieces*, Yale University Press, New Haven.

National Children's Home (NCH), 2002, *Factfile 2002–2003*, NCH Publications, London.

Okri B, 1991, *The Famished Road*, Cape, London.

Orbach S, 1994, *What's Really Going On Here?*, Virago, London.

Ovid, 1995, *Orpheus in the Underworld*, Innes M (trans), Penguin, Harmondsworth. (Original work published 1955.)

Padel R, 1995, *Whom Gods Destroy: Elements of Greek and Tragic Madness*, Princeton University Press, Princeton, NJ.

Panksepp J, 1998, *Affective Neuroscience*, Oxford University Press, Oxford.

Panksepp J, 2001, 'The Long-Term Psychobiological Consequences of Infant Emotions: Prescriptions for the Twenty-First Century', Schore A (ed), *Infant Mental Health Journal 22*, pp132–62.

Pinter H, 1991, *Collected Poems and Prose*, Faber & Faber, London.

Reid S, 1992, *Understanding Your 2 Year Old*, Rosendale, London.

Resnick B, 1993, 'Couples Psychotherapy', Lecture, Metanoia Psychotherapy Training Institute, London.

Robbins A, 1986, *Unlimited Power: The New Science of Personal Achievement*, Simon & Schuster, New York.

Rosenfeld H, 1965, *Psychotic States: A Psychoanalytical Approach*, Maresfield Library, London.

Rowan J, 1990, *Subpersonalities: The People Inside Us*, Routledge, London.

Rowe D, 1988, *The Successful Self*, Fontana, London.

Scurfield R, 1985, 'Post Trauma Stress Assessment and Treatment: Overview and Formulations', Figley C (ed), *Trauma and its Wake*, Brunner/Mazel, New York, pp219–56.

Segal J, 1985, *Phantasy in Everyday Life: A Psychoanalytical Approach to Understanding Ourselves*, Penguin, Harmondsworth.

Steiner J, 1993, *Psychic Retreats: Pathological Organizations in Psychotic, Neurotic and Borderline Patients*, Routledge/Institute of Psychoanalysis, London.

Sunderland M, 2003, *Teenie Weenie in a Too Big World*, Speechmark Publishing, Bicester.

Thrail E, 1994, *Retrospect: The Story of an Analysis*, Quartet, London.

Waitley D, 1985, *Seeds of Greatness: The Ten Best-Kept Secrets of Total Success*, Cedar, London.

Wickes FG, 1976, *The Inner World of Choice*, 3rd edn, Englewood Cliffs, New York. (Original work published 1963.)

Williams G, 1997, *Internal Landscapes and Foreign Bodies: Eating Disorders and Other Pathologies*, Karnac Books, London.

Williamson M, 1992, *A Return to Love*, Random House, New York.

Winnicott DW, 1965, 'The Capacity to be Alone', *The Maturational Process and the Facilitating Environment*, Hogarth, London, pp29–36. (Original work published 1958.)

Winnicott DW, 1965, *The Maturational Process and the Facilitating Environment*, Hogarth, London.